Pr

"For the past decade, I have had the pleasure of a front row seat observing Ben Sporer putting his expertise into action. Ben's ability to guide individuals, groups, teams, and organizations to look within themselves to find and develop their high-performance plan is proven and impressive. Whether we're on the field, in the office, or out helping our communities, this playbook gives us the framework to discover our next higher level and beyond."

JEFF MALLETT, founding president of Yahoo! and co-owner of Vancouver Whitecaps FC

"I have worked with over fifty Olympic medalists. This book will not only give you their winning recipe, but it will also show you how to apply it to your career and everyday life. Ben Sporer is one of the best in his domain because he is a master at simplifying and customizing his approach. When reading *Output*, this is exactly what I felt: Ben found a way for every reader to capture and apply key performance concepts to their reality. As an individual, you will find the map to your true potential. As a leader, you will acquire tools to help others reach theirs."

DOMINICK GAUTHIER, co-founder and COO of B2ten, Olympian and Olympic coach, and media personality

"Working with Ben Sporer these past fifteen years has optimized my performance both on the bike and in the boardroom. Ben has been able to maximize my output and, in turn, my results."

BRIAN HILL, founder and executive chair of Aritzia

"It's thrilling to read the details that break down how Ben Sporer helped my snowboard career in a period when his leadership catapulted the success rate of the Canadian snowboard cross team performances. Reading *Output* instantly ignited my desire to be back at the 2010 Olympic Games, on top of Cypress Mountain, knowing we were prepared to perform, all orchestrated by our maestro Ben. The lessons learned in this book have already given me ideas to elevate my work as a coach and as a parent."

MAËLLE RICKER, Olympic gold medalist and national team co-head coach of Canada Snowboard

"Having had the privilege to work with Ben Sporer for over fifteen years, I have consistently increased my output athletically, professionally, and personally. Ben's approach has had a major impact on the culture of my organization, my fitness goals, and my desire to increase my overall daily performance! Doing the work is essential, but a comprehensive plan will ensure you meet or exceed your full potential."

JOHN HORTON, president and CEO of SHAPE

"Late into my first season playing in the NHL, I realized that my overall preparation and training regimen needed to change if I wanted to reach my maximum potential. That summer, I met Ben Sporer. Ben's approach to the human body and high performance has greatly improved both my life and my career. He is able to zero in on goals by setting up the clear and definitive programs needed to achieve them."

SAM REINHART, NHL hockey player for the Florida Panthers

"In *Output*, Ben Sporer introduces a paradigm shift that has the potential to revolutionize the performance industry. Drawing on my twenty years of experience in executive and leadership performance, I recognize the transformative power of focusing on output rather than outcome. This innovative approach will not only reshape the way performers approach their craft but also transform the work of those who support them. As a CEO, executive leadership consultant, and combat veteran military officer, I have encountered various strategies and frameworks to optimize performance. However, *Output* by Ben Sporer stands out as an indispensable resource for individuals who are truly dedicated to achieving peak performance. It has already changed the way I approach my work, and I am excited to see the far-reaching impact this book will have on the industry as a whole."

KARI GRANGER, founding partner and CEO of The Granger Network

"Ben Sporer has done something really special with *Output*: demystifying complex scientific insight and sharing his extensive experience with high performers in sport and business. With the set of principles in this book, any reader can learn to define their desired performance and achieve it sustainably. *Output* is a gift for business leaders to learn how to utilize sport-performance principles to create a higher level of sustained performance. It is a gift for athletes to take agency over their performance and get the most out of their team. This book contains everything you need, and nothing you don't, for anyone aiming to do anything extraordinary!"

JEREMY SHEPPARD, PhD, director of health and athletic performance at Canada Snowboard

"Ben Sporer, one of Canada's leaders in human performance, has taken what is complex and complicated and made it simple and pragmatic. In a world full of the next buzz word, technological trend, and artificial intelligence, having a compass like *Output* to provide you with direction for your own high-performing life is invaluable."

SCOTT LIVINGSTON, host of *Leave Your Mark* podcast, co-founder of Reconditioning HQ, and president of High Performance Consultants

"Through years of coaching and training, Ben Sporer has helped instil many of the same principles from *Output* that I utilize in my athletic performance as well as in my daily life. Performance is a product of process, and Ben articulates that very well. *Output* is an inspiring must-read for anyone wanting a deeper look and understanding into the process of a high-performance athlete."

FINN ILES, World Cup downhill mountain bike racer

"'Performance can be simplified, but that doesn't mean that it is easy.' In this observation, Ben Sporer captures the essence of his succinct examination of performance and his revealing discussion around the supporting constructs of outcome and output. Ben lays out a clear description and opinion concerning critical factors for executing on the objectives characteristic of any high-performance pursuit. *Output* is required reading for all those interested in this fascinating and compelling topic."

STEPHEN NORRIS, PhD, performance development consultant

OUTPUT

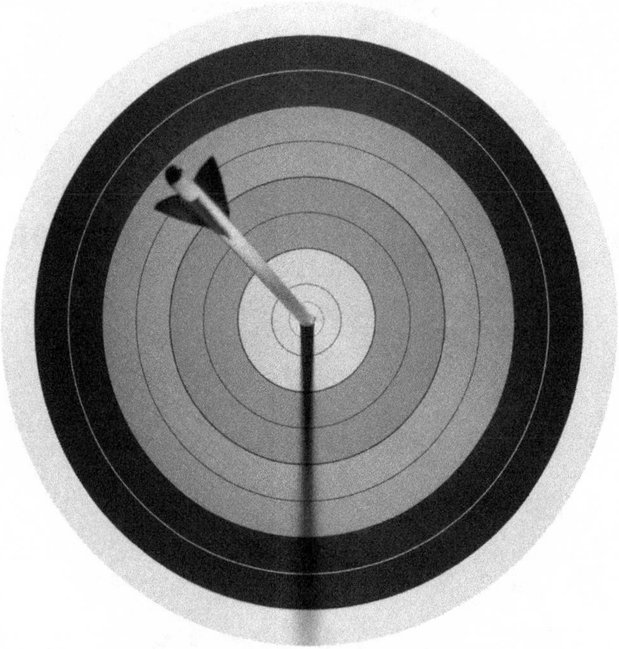

OUTPUT

OPTIMIZING YOUR PERFORMANCE WITH LESSONS LEARNED FROM SPORT

BEN SPORER PhD

PAGE TWO

Some names and identifying details have been changed to protect the privacy of individuals.

This book is not intended as a substitute for the medical advice of physicians. The reader should regularly consult a physician in matters relating to his/her/their health and particularly with respect to any symptoms that may require diagnosis or medical attention.

Cataloguing in publication information is available from Library and Archives Canada.

ISBN 978-1-77458-424-8 (Paperback)
ISBN 978-1-77458-425-5 (Ebook)

Page Two
pagetwo.com

Edited by Scott Steedman
Copyedited by Melissa Edwards
Proofread by Jenny Govier
Cover and interior design by Cameron McKague

www.output-book.com

This is dedicated to high performers
and to those individuals who aren't there yet.
You inspire me to learn, grow, and share.

Contents

INTRODUCTION

What Is Required for High Performance?

It is not to see something first, but to establish solid connections between the previously known and the hitherto unknown that constitutes the essence of scientific discovery. It is this process of tying together which can best promote true understanding and real progress.

HANS SELYE, MD, *The Stress of Life*

ELITE ATHLETES deliver and perform under pressure. We watch in awe as Olympians and major-league players execute incredible levels of skill, strength, strategy, focus, and teamwork, not just in one culminating moment but again and again over years of a distinguished career, or in grueling annual schedules that have them traveling across the continent to play sometimes more than a hundred games in a season. What you likely don't realize is that these athletes are not different from you. We all have to show up every day and perform at what we do, again and again and again. And we all have the ability to deliver that performance at an excellent level, if we are willing to do what is required of us.

But what exactly *is* required for high performance—and how do you even define it? If you ask a hundred people what attributes you need, you'll likely get a hundred different answers. Some will point to natural talent, others to genetics, other still to a rigorous work ethic, boundless energy, or the ability to make quick decisions. In a given situation, any of these answers might be correct. But to deliver consistent high performance, on demand, you can't rely solely on talent or tactics. And to measure that high performance, you can't look to wins or records.

Why? Because performance is not outcome. It's output.

As a physiologist, I look at the world through a systems approach. How are ideas related? How does one thing influence another? What I've come to learn over my career is that the core attributes of performance are like the gears in a clock, working together to deliver the precise output that is needed to obtain an objective, no matter what that objective is. Using this larger perspective, I help clients succeed by working with them to design an integrated, personalized performance plan that connects their desired objective with the specific output that is required for them to execute the performance and obtain that objective.

I first connected with my desire to work in high-performance sport when I was traveling in Australia in my early twenties, looking for work as a systems analyst after earning my diploma in computer science. In my time there I had many opportunities to watch sports that were totally new to me: Aussie rules football, rugby union, rugby league, and, most interesting of all to me back then, cricket. In Sydney, I had the chance to catch a game at a cricket ground in a beautiful spot called Coogee Bay. From my vantage point in the stands, I tried to decipher how it all worked: *So those are the wickets; that's where the guy throws the ball; ah, the bowler runs up like that; wow, the fielders catch that hard red ball with their bare hands*... I remember thinking to myself that I just loved sports and competition, period. I also realized that I had an ability to figure out quickly how a sport worked, and why a given player was able to be successful.

A few days before that cricket game, I had managed to get a cheap student ticket to see a virtuoso violinist at the Sydney Opera House. It was not my usual thing—I had never been into classical music—but I found myself blown away by how skilled this musician was at playing the violin. I sat there in that famous concert hall feeling amazed that people can become so good at doing what they do. And not merely good, but great.

Behind the soloist I could see all of the other violinists in the orchestra—and, of course, they were also very skilled. And yet they were there to back up someone who had flown in from another continent, someone who was clearly far better than any of them. I sat there watching her coax these sounds out of her instrument, feeling fascinated by the concept of high performance. How did she become so good at this? I wanted to know more about the pursuit of excellence, and I wanted to be around that pursuit all the time.

I never did continue as a systems analyst—although the work I do now does involve analyzing systems. Back home in Canada, with some basic science courses under my belt, I found myself at the University of Victoria listening to a lecture by a professor of physiology named Dr. Howie Wenger. He was also a consultant in the NHL at the time, working with a few different teams, and his lecture confirmed for me that I had found my calling (and, as it turns out, I had also found a mentor and lifelong friend). He later became my advisor as I earned my master's degree, and through that process he opened doors for me into the world of elite, high-performance sport, where I have been working ever since.

Studying human physiology with Dr. Wenger, I learned to see how systems function together. We undertook research to understand how, in every situation, inputs relate to outputs. Yes, strength training will make you stronger, but each person will respond to the same stimulus differently, and some won't respond at all. Sometimes aerobic and strength work will interfere with each other and compromise gains from one or the other. In other cases, they won't; you get zero interference and the two are complementary.

Dr. Wenger taught me valuable lessons in interpreting, understanding, and respecting science, but he also challenged me to think critically about information, and to appreciate the art of applying science to everyday situations. Scientific researchers must be careful that their inferences in data are relative to the controls that are put in place in the study. Is everyone on the same diet? Are they getting the same amount of sleep? Do they have a similar genetic makeup? If not, how has that influenced the individual results? As scientific researchers and practitioners, we have to appreciate that individuals are unique, and that there is always individual context in which we are trying to apply our work. Every person will have different genetics, training history, backgrounds, support structures, likes, and dislikes. Humans are systems, and stimuli and responses do not occur in isolation from one another. Neither do the factors that determine performance output.

Physiology has been the ideal path for me to understand performance, because it uses a systems view to study how the body functions. It's a very integrated approach. You can't think about building muscle without thinking about how muscles are impacted by the nervous system, the endocrine system, and so on—any one action will have knock-on effects on different physiological systems. How well do you recover from the work? Do you overstress the muscle, or understress it? How much time do you have to recover, and are you providing the fuel you need for the muscle to adapt properly? It's all connected, integrated.

My first full-time job as a physiologist working in sports was with an institute called Pacific Sport, which eventually became one of the Canadian Sports Institutes. They were working to develop the concept of a

True high performance on demand is not a short-term thing: **you have to plan a way to achieve it in a realistic, sustainable way.**

high-performance sport model, similar to what Australia was doing. Eventually, I became one of the first full-time physiologists to work solely on Olympic sport in Canada. Taking the learnings from working with Dr. Wenger, I began working with athletes, critically thinking about their challenges and the factors that drive their personal performance, and how to get the most out of their efforts. Now, alongside that work, I am translating this same process to help executives and other professionals in the non-sport world achieve their goals, too. These concepts apply in exactly the same way for those executive worlds, as they do for whatever world you operate in. In fact, they can be applied to anyone who wants to learn and isn't afraid of hard work.

And yet, for so many, the path forward to high performance still seems so unclear. When people learn what it is that I do, I often hear the same question: "What is it that makes elite athletes different?" In other words, "Why are those athletes able to perform on demand at such a high level, and how can I do the same thing?" The truth is that there are many ways to achieve high performance. In this book, I offer a path that will allow you to change your understanding of performance itself. It is a distillation of the experience and insight of all the coaches, athletes, colleagues, and executives who I have worked with over my career.

There are so many studies and so much anecdotal information out there about achieving excellence, and it is easy to get overwhelmed. How do you fit it all in and sort through all of the conflicting directions? My hope is to cut through the conflicting clutter of advice out there, so that you can develop a simple, clear plan that is tailored to your specific needs—whatever those needs may be. In the end, the formula is simple: you have to focus on output, not outcome. Your output will be determined by your preparation. Your preparation must be an integrated performance plan. And that plan must be individual, specific, and purposeful.

This book will give you the knowledge you need to prioritize your choices, so you can be strategic about where to focus your efforts. Consistent high performance on demand is not a short-term thing: you have to plan a way to achieve it in a realistic, sustainable way.

And there lies one of the biggest challenges I see in sport: a lack of ownership for developing a clear, integrated performance strategy. I often see athletes, coaches, and leaders simply drive forward, assuming that everyone they work with is already aligned around their performance objective. These people can be committed, skilled, hardworking, accountable—but they are not taking ownership to develop a clear performance objective, to communicate that objective, and to build a tailored solution that matches their current context. Some athletes and coaches rely on what they have seen work for others without first considering the context and if it's appropriate for them. I see the same mistakes play out in the executive world, and in every field and profession I come into contact with through my work. It was this recurring theme that made me realize that the factors and pitfalls that influence high performance are the same, regardless of the field.

I'm not here to provide you with a long list of research studies or to explain complex scientific theories. What I will do is combine my scientific training and years of experience in Olympic and professional sport to examine and simplify the complexities and moving gears of high performance into a process that is doable, plannable, and personalized. I will challenge you to rethink your own performance and see that you can also be a high performer on demand when it matters. This doesn't mean that high performance can be simple or easy—but it does mean that, when you have a focused and clear plan, it is within your grasp.

In his performance career, the great triathlete Simon Whitfield embodied what he called "the relentless pursuit of excellence," and he also expected that same relentless pursuit from everyone around him. How can you get the most out of what you're doing so that you can be better than you are right now and sustain a high level of performance in whatever area you choose? You don't have to do everything. But the process starts with acknowledging that something's going to change, and understanding that the aspects of performance all influence each other. Your actions in one area of your life will impact other areas. You can't be at the top of your game every day, but you can sustainably raise your level of performance on demand, so that even when you're tired, your performance will be better than it was before. That, in itself, is relentless pursuit.

This book is for anyone who wants to learn to perform better. Get on a path. Give yourself permission to own it. You *can* deliver, day in and day out.

PART 1

RETHINKING PERFORMANCE

1

Performance Is Output, Not Outcome

There is a gate between process and outcome.
Output is the key that unlocks that gate.

WAITING AT the starting gate on his bike, Finn Iles is ready. The twenty-two-year-old Canadian downhill mountain biker from Pemberton, British Columbia, is poised at the top of a rocky course on the treed slopes of Mont-Sainte-Anne, Quebec. It is August 6, 2022, and Finn is about to compete in one of the biggest races of his life, on home soil. He had clocked the fastest time in the qualifying rounds, so he is scheduled to go down last. But the competition he is facing is formidable: one of the first racers, Britain's Laurie Greenland, laid down a run seven seconds faster than anyone else's in the race so far and six seconds faster than Finn's qualifying run. If Finn wants to win his first Elite Men's World Cup race, he is going to have to beat that time.

Mont-Sainte-Anne is the only World Cup mountain biking race in Canada, and a big crowd has gathered to cheer on their countryman. Finn knows he has to go faster than he ever has before—and from the very first moment, he delivers. At the first split—a racing term for a distance marker—his time is already better than any of the competitors who went before him. And he keeps up that pace, hurtling down the course and extending his lead at the second split.

Then, with less than half the race to go, catastrophe strikes: the chain on Finn's bike breaks.

At a moment like this, many other riders would panic or simply stop racing. Finn, however, knows what to do. He can't pedal, but he can adjust his stance, tucking his body in and using gravity and momentum to sustain his speed. He has the entire course already mapped out in his head, which allows him to maintain speed at the right moments, and choose the optimal line on every corner. He isn't going as quickly as he would if he could pedal, but he continues down the hill just fast enough to cross the finish line 0.238 seconds ahead of Laurie Greenland.

The gathered crowd erupts in joy. Finn is overcome with emotion as he hugs his parents and friends. With this victory, he has become only the second Canadian in history to win an elite World Cup, and the first since the legendary Stevie Smith accomplished the feat a full nine years earlier. And he did it on home soil, with his family and thousands of his fans there to watch.

Finn Iles's victory at Mont-Sainte-Anne wasn't just high performance in action. It was high performance on demand, right when it mattered most.

It's an impressive enough accomplishment on its own, but it's even more so when you add in the fact that Finn had to change his game plan on the fly after his chain broke. The race only lasted three and a half minutes, but for a rider, that's an eternity. As he rode, Finn was processing all the information around him at a rapid speed, calculating and strategizing and adjusting his angles and body position. He was going really fast—peaking over 60 kilometers an hour, riding over rocks and past trees on an extremely steep slope. To Finn, though, it didn't *feel* fast. From a spectator's perspective, an elite downhill mountain bike run looks chaotic and out of control, but to the person on the bike it is anything but. At every moment, Finn had complete command, putting in the performance of his life, getting his bike down that hill faster than anyone else in the world, when and where it mattered.

That's high performance.

What Is Performance?

What do people mean when they talk about performance? We often hear the word used as a catch-all for so many things, in and outside the world of sports: you see it in job titles and coaching departments; you hear it referred to when teams or individuals are talking about their goals or objectives. A young athlete might have a performance goal of becoming an MVP—a most valuable player—or making it to the major leagues. A young professional might have a performance goal of making it to the C-suite or starting their own business, or even becoming a super parent while holding down a career. But while goals like these are important, they are the performance *outcome*, not the performance itself. If you want to truly understand performance, you can't evaluate it just on the end result—on whether or not you achieved your goal. You have to evaluate it on your *output*.

Performance is not about what you want to achieve. It is about how well you can execute what you need to do to achieve it—in other words, what you do to create the desired output. Are you able to execute and integrate the critical components in your field of play—whether that is sport or business or parenting or art—well enough to produce an output that increases your chance of being successful? Can you master everything that is in your control, and, most importantly, do so on demand?

This is performance—the act of producing an integrated output between the start and end whistles. So when we speak about optimizing performance, we must speak about optimizing our ability to produce that output, not about what we want to achieve by it. And when we evaluate our performance, we must evaluate it against our optimal output, not our optimal outcome.

How Is Output Different from Outcome?

Your output is a big part of your outcome, but it is not the only part. Think of a game of soccer. For ninety minutes (and sometimes more), eleven players on one team take the field to play against eleven players on another team. The referee blows the whistle to start the game, and again to end it. The *outcome* is the score, and whether one team won or lost. The *output* is what actually happens on the field during those ninety-plus minutes of play. There are so many factors that could affect the outcome—the referee could make a bad call and award a goal to a team that should have been called off for a handball; an extreme windstorm in the second half could favor one team and allow them to score goals while making it extremely difficult for the other team to get in the offensive zone; and any number of other preventable or unpredictable elements could come into play. None of those factors have anything to do with how well the players on either team played, or how well they were coached to play together as a team.

In sport, if you want to evaluate the performance of an individual player and the team as a whole, you first have to be clear on what your expectations are for that match or that competition or that series of competitions, both for each player and for the team. What are the team tactics? How do they execute those tactics as a team? How do they execute them as individuals? What skills do the team, and each individual player—the goalkeeper, a central defender, a striker—need to express? And, just like

If you want to truly understand performance, you can't evaluate it just on the end result . . .
You have to evaluate it on your *output*.

with the tactics, how do the players execute those skills as individuals, and how do they execute them together as a group? How often are they expected to do that?

A well-coached defender playing within that team's tactics, for example, will know what's expected of them whenever they have 20 meters of free space in front of them: they know that their coach will want them to move up the pitch into that space. They will also know that if they don't have that space, they should pass the ball. If that defender gets to the halfway line, one of the midfielders will know to run into a channel for a forward pass. The coaching team can only evaluate the performance of the team and of each of those players if they have clearly articulated all of these expectations to all of the players, and if they are able to measure them accurately at the end of the match.

If there was a refereeing error during this game, a team that had a very successful performance (output) could still face an undesirable result (outcome). Output is not the same as outcome. You could have one of the best performances of your season, or even of your career, and still lose the game. (Or not get the promotion, or not land the contract.) The other team's goalie could have the game of their life, making nine saves, two of them extraordinary. You can't control that.

Alternatively, you can play poorly and still win. Maybe the team you played wasn't well prepared and couldn't get a shot on goal. Maybe they had thirty shots—a large number!—but missed the net or were blocked on twenty-eight of them and hit the post twice. Again, you can't control any of that. You also can't control the fact that their goalie fumbled a back pass into the feet of your striker, who scuffed the ball into the net to let you win 1–0. Your performance (your output) was poor, but your result (your outcome) was very favorable. Sure, when you and your fellow players collect your championship medals and spray each other with champagne, you don't care! But a good coach will know that it was not any kind of great performance from your team that won the game. It was luck, and a poor performance from your competitors.

What's important is to make sure that when you're evaluating your performance, you do so against expectations, and that you are honest with yourself and don't take credit for the lucky wins you didn't deserve. Instead, you must evaluate all of your performances, be they lucky wins or unlucky losses, based on a series of clearly defined metrics that relate to your expectations of output.

PERFORMANCE, OUTCOME, AND OUTPUT

PERFORMANCE: The execution of a task or function. Performance is an action.

OUTCOME: The way things turn out, based on factors inside and outside your control. Outcome is the result.

OUTPUT: An expression of your efforts based on things you can control. Output is what you deliver in your performance.

How Is Output Different from Process?

When I tell you to focus on your execution rather than your goal or outcome, you might be thinking that I am talking simply about *process*: the series of specific steps you need to take to complete a particular task or achieve a desired end. But while process is foundational to success, focusing only on the steps you need to take can actually be detrimental to that success—especially if they aren't the right steps.

Say you want to make a beautiful chocolate cake, so you find a recipe for it on the internet. You might assume that if you follow that recipe exactly, you will deliver the cake you expect. But if that recipe is wrong—if the steps you're following are not the right steps—you will not get the cake you want. Output is not about delivering a product—or, more specifically, it is not about delivering just *any* product. It is about delivering the right product to achieve the objective.

I see this play out often in elite sport: an individual becomes so focused on the process that they lose track of the output that is required to achieve their goal. They are committed to their preparation, but they are not developing the ability to deliver the right output on demand in high-pressure environments. In sport, like in so many fields, the goal almost always relates to winning. But if you want to win, you can't focus solely on *winning*—you have to focus on delivering the output that is required to win. You may think this is just semantics, but the difference between the two is important to understand. There is a gate between process and outcome. Output is the key that unlocks that gate.

Take that chocolate cake: if you were entering a local baking contest and you really wanted your cake to win (outcome), you would first bring out your favorite recipe and ingredients (process). The steps are clearly written out, you have all the tools and materials you need on your baking counter, and if you follow the recipe correctly, you will eventually end up with something that looks, feels, and tastes like chocolate cake (output).

But will all recipes lead to the same chocolate cake, or will some recipes lead to a better chocolate cake? We'd all likely agree that no, the cakes will not be the same, and yes, some will be better than others. So now let's say that, to increase your chances of winning, you practiced multiple times with multiple recipes (process in preparation), and followed each recipe exactly as written—in other words, you executed the process perfectly. But among all of those chocolate cakes—the different types of output—which recipe delivered the *best* chocolate cake, the one that will win the contest?

That's where it gets complicated, because the answer depends on who is judging the cakes and what criteria they are using: taste, consistency, moistness, looks. So to *increase the likelihood* of producing a winner (outcome) you first need to clearly define the attributes of a winning cake (output) and which recipe you would need to follow (process in execution) to produce a cake with those exact qualities. You need to ask yourself this: *What is the required output I must produce that will get me to my desired outcome?*

Output is not the same as outcome. You could have one of the best performances of your season, or even of your career, and still lose the game.

It is so important here to be very honest and very specific about your performance objective and the output required to achieve it. This is the one thing you have control over—yet it is also where most people fall short. Despite the praise we give our champions, we as a society often seem to have an aversion to hearing people talk about actually putting their focus on *winning* rather than *trying*. We often tell people to prioritize process, and to worry less about winning. But the truth is that high performers do want to win—in whatever way they are defining that word. So the message that winning is not important is doing a disservice.

If you want to be the best at whatever it is that you do, you have to be comfortable enough with that desire to own it, and to articulate it. That honesty will help you focus on the specific output required to reach your objective, and to do the required work that will put you in a place where you can produce that required output on demand. Just remember that *winning* is a much broader term than how most people define it. If your goal is to be your personal best, and you reach that goal, then you have won, regardless of what a personal best looks like for other people.

WHAT IS PROCESS, EXACTLY?

In my work with athletes and coaches, I often hear people referring to process as one of two things: either the steps an athlete will focus on during their actual performance, or the steps they will focus on during their preparation and training.

The first definition is about process in execution—it is task-oriented. For a snowboard cross racer, for example, it might be about executing their race strategy, focusing on the start, sticking to the same line they have practiced, using proper edging technique, and using the right jump takeoff and landing positions. If you were making that chocolate cake, it would be about following the recipe perfectly, making sure the measurements are precise, and setting the right temperature on the oven.

The second definition—the steps an athlete focuses on during training—relates to all the things that athlete would do over the long term to prepare for their event—it is process in preparation. For our snowboard cross racer, this would include the work they do in the gym to build the strength to be able to tolerate the impacts, the conditioning to reduce their fatigue during competition, the on-snow racing that lets them work on tactical aspects or build the mindset that will help them dig deep in competition when it matters, or the hundreds of runs they do to perfect their edging. These longer-term investments help the athlete improve their capacity to deliver on the required output. For a chocolate cake, this would be the time you spend over years perfecting the way you whisk an egg, the knowledge you build about the idiosyncrasies of a specific oven's temperature or humidity, or the setup you use to prepare for an efficient baking process.

When I talk about process in this book, for the most part I am referring to the longer-term context. But both interpretations of process are important.

It is worth repeating that you have no control over the outcome. In sports, the way a thing turns out is often binary: win or lose. Good preparation will give you the required output and increase your odds of a sustained high performance and your preferred outcome. But you still might not win. The judge at that bake-off might not choose your cake, even after you clearly identified the required output and executed on delivering the most delicious and beautiful cake you've ever made. In the end, you might be beaten by a late entry from a world-class chef with thirty years' experience in refining their cake-making craft. Or maybe the judge they appointed just didn't like the taste or look of your cake. You set a high expectation for yourself and your output met that expectation. You had a high performance but you didn't take home the prize. It happens. That's why you measure performance against the output, not against the outcome.

Defining Your Output

If you want to achieve your goals, it's important that you clearly understand what output will be required from you. You need to be specific, as this understanding will form the basis for both your preparation for and the evaluation of your performance. This is about determining both the attributes and the level of execution you will require if you want to be successful.

Take for example a cyclist who wants to win a gold medal in the pursuit at the Olympics. The cyclist's first step is to define the output they need to win that medal. What time do they need to beat? What is the average power output that will achieve that time? What is the best pacing strategy? What is the mindset that will allow them to deliver that output when their body is in agony and is telling them to stop? What do they need to do in each moment to be successful? That is the required output.

You might be wondering how the work a cyclist does to define the output they need to win an Olympic medal would apply to business, or to any other non-athletic objective you might want to accomplish in your life. Well, for any given objective, the required output might be different, but the principles are the same. If you are an entrepreneur who wants your new startup to be successful in the marketplace, for example, the individual output that will be required of you might be to show up to work with good energy, to lead your organization, and to make quality decisions under pressure. And while an athlete will only have to meet their highest output capacity levels during a competition period, you may have to meet these requirements for seventy-plus hours per week, every week of the year.

That brings us to another important element of performance: once you've defined your required output, you need to evaluate your own personal profile and have an honest look at your ability to produce it. Do you have the capacity for that effort? Do you have the skills that output will require of you, and will you be able to execute and integrate them well enough in your field of play to produce an output that increases your chances of success? Can you master everything in your control, and do it on demand?

Lesson Learned

Human performance is the ultimate execution of your goals to meet an objective. It is an *output*, not an *outcome*. This is true not just for sport but for any and every aspect of your life. To perform in a way that is sustainable over time, you have to think critically about the decisions and factors that influence your output.

2

The Core 4

All performances have physical, mental, technical, and tactical aspects.

THERE ARE hundreds—perhaps thousands—of factors that can either lead to an optimal output or set it out of reach. Recently, I was reviewing a post from a colleague that identified over thirty items that influence performance to varying degrees. And this was a short list! One of those thirty items was fatigue, and in a subsequent post the author listed thirty-plus further items that could influence fatigue.

The endless range of influences over performance is mindboggling, as is the endless range of ways you can describe them. So, among this sea of variables, how can you begin to identify the key factors that can help you produce the output that is required of you?

The best way to start is by organizing those influences. The vast majority of performance factors can be bundled into four categories, which I call the Core 4:

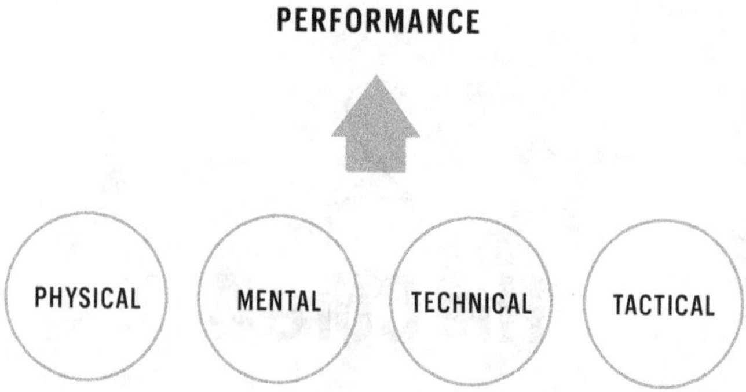

The Core 4

I have had a long career in athletic performance that has spanned multiple sports at multiple levels, and I have since spent many years applying similar strategies and principles in my work training business executives and entrepreneurs. And in all that time I have found that the Core 4 framework—physical, mental, technical, and tactical factors, all contributing to the overall output—applies almost universally to performance in any environment. The only thing that varies is the relative importance of each category.

It's true: if you take the time to dissect the output, *all* human performance can be broken down into the Core 4, whether that's in a music hall, arena, or stadium; on stage; at home; or in the workplace. *All* human performance relies on and is affected by the Core 4.

There are libraries of insightful books written by sport, business, and scientific experts that delve into the many hundreds of secondary factors that influence each of these four main categories. For the purposes of this chapter, I'm going to offer a high-level look at how each of the Core 4 factors can affect your performance in any pursuit you are taking on.

Physical Factors

When people think about sports and athletics, they often associate it with the traits they think make up the physical components of sport: they picture an athlete and see someone who is super fit, strong, in great shape, fast, muscular, explosive, or able to run forever and never tire. Without question, these physical attributes are a key component of any athlete's overall performance. In terms of the Core 4 and how they apply to all forms of performance, this category includes anything that relates to the physical ability of your body to produce the required output.

The obvious physical attributes are the basic components of health and fitness, including functional movement, muscular strength, endurance, power, energy systems, and flexibility. Each of these could be further broken down into its subcomponents—for example, strength can be subdivided into maximal (the amount you can lift for one to three repetitions), endurance (typically fifteen or more repetitions), speed strength (how much you can lift at a fast speed), strength speed (how fast you can move a relatively heavy load), and even body weight strength. Likewise, energy systems can be divided into aerobic (using oxygen) and anaerobic (without oxygen) subcomponents, and further broken down into the categories of power (the maximal rate at which energy can be produced by a specific energy system) or capacity (the total amount of work that can be completed using a specific energy system). The level of detail that is required depends on both the importance of that attribute to the specific performance and the output required for the specific objective. For example, the level needed for aerobic energy system development will be very different between a marathon runner and a hockey player, and very different again between Olympic and amateur marathon runners. It will also be different for an executive who travels over a hundred days per year versus one who doesn't travel at all.

To win his World Cup race, Finn Iles needed to perform many physical tasks at the highest level. He needed power to get out of the start gate quickly, to get up to speed early on the course, and to accelerate out of corners all the way down. He needed muscular endurance to handle the bounces as he rolled over bumpy terrain, and to hold the tuck position for an extended time after his chain broke (something that would have been very difficult to sustain with no resistance on the pedals). His legs and shoulders also needed a significant level of what is called "eccentric strength" to absorb big impacts on compression when he landed off drops or when he was coming out of steep, technical sections. His balance and core strength each played a key role in maintaining his body position while he took corners and while he was maneuvering the bike underneath him. Lastly, he needed a level of conditioning that allowed him to maintain his output for close to four minutes without succumbing to fatigue.

While the physical requirements may not seem as obvious for non-sport performers, they still play a role in achieving sustainable high performance. Consider the entrepreneur who is trying to launch a new company. They need the physical capacity to handle long days at the office, to help minimize fatigue, or to better deal with travel load and jet lag. They may be required to sit at a computer or desk for long hours, and so they must maintain a certain level of mobility and core strength to prevent back, neck, or postural problems, each of which could have a negative impact on their ability to deliver on their output. Yes, these are very different from the physical aspects required by an elite athlete, but they are still important to delivering sustained performance.

EXAMPLES OF PHYSICAL FACTORS

MOUNTAIN BIKING: Aerobic conditioning for endurance; upper body strength to control your bike; leg power to get up a steep technical section

ICE HOCKEY: Ability to play twenty minutes a night with intense effort; ability to recover between shifts; upper body strength to battle against the boards; adequate flexibility with hip range of motion to prevent injury; stamina to withstand many hours of training

BUSINESS: Capacity to sustain a busy schedule and handle travel fatigue; health maintenance; ability to recover quickly over back-to-back long days; ability to sit at computer and minimize back injuries

MUSIC: Ability to play a two-hour concert night after night; ability to dance and project your voice; stamina to travel between cities and venues

Mental Factors

Mental factors that impact performance include anything related to the mind and how it can influence your output. When you watch a high performer, what might stand out to you is their poise and focus: they rarely seem to be rattled by the pressure and public attention that is being piled onto them. Coaches often want to see athletes who are mentally tough and robust, and who can stay resilient when things go wrong. They'll talk about looking for "competitors" who "just know how to win." For some athletes, this mindset is almost instinctive, while for others, it is a deliberate and critical process that they have adopted. Through conscious practice, they are able to put themselves into a performance-on-demand state.

For Finn's World Cup performance, there were several mental factors that contributed to his output. Before he even entered the start gate, he had to block out any life distractions outside of racing in order to free up his mental capacity and remain focused on the task at hand.

As he waited at the gate, he was almost certainly performing his pre-race routine in his mind, visualizing himself running through the entire course while tracing the optimal lines in his head. He knew he was the last rider down the hill, and that the current leader in the race had already beaten his best time by over six seconds. Along with that pressure, he had to handle the knowledge that he was competing on home soil in front of thousands of fans who were desperate for him to win, and he had to block out all the unwanted and distracting comments those same well-meaning onlookers were shouting at him as he waited in the start gate.

And that was all before the race began. On the course, Finn had to remain focused as he sped over and by obstacles at speeds of up to 60 kilometers per hour, with any miscalculation potentially leading to a disastrous crash. If he missed a line or carried too much speed into a stretch, he had to process that information instantly and make rapid-fire decisions and adjustments. And after all that planning and repetitive visualization, he had to change his tactics instantaneously when his chain broke, and remain totally focused through the full last third of the race, knowing that he was carrying enough speed to possibly win if he made the right adjustments. It would have been easy to give up, but he didn't. He delivered the output and he won.

In non-sport environments, the mental aspects of performance are often more obvious. Imagine the musician or actor who stands on stage to perform in front of thousands of people while flawlessly delivering a complicated

All human performance relies on and is affected by the Core 4.

piece. These performers practice over and over, rehearsing and visualizing to make sure they perfect their craft and delivery. They can remain focused throughout their performance even when something goes wrong, and they do it so well that the audience is often unaware. And in recent years, we all witnessed an increase in our required mental aspects during the COVID-19 pandemic. Uncertainty, fear, anxiety, stress, and grief (and so much more) came into every moment of our daily lives. Unpredictable pressures were put on nearly everyone, at nearly all levels. The pandemic, with all of its stressors and tragedies, was a window into how all of us, collectively and individually, manage and handle pressures in different ways.

EXAMPLES OF MENTAL FACTORS

MOUNTAIN BIKING: Performance visualization before a competition; focus during a race; confidence in your abilities

ICE HOCKEY: Managing pressure; confidence in your abilities; trust in your partner or team; maintaining focus on your output

BUSINESS: Stress management; ability to relax; making decisions under pressure; maintaining focus during meetings and presentations; handling deadline pressure; confidence in your abilities and in your pitches

MUSIC: Overcoming stage fright; coping with time away from family; ability to focus during distractions; visualization to prepare for a performance

Technical Factors

People often describe top athletes as either possessing great technical skill or being highly talented and born with a gift—and sometimes they describe them as both. There is some truth to each of these ideas, but they are also both misleading. Every high performer requires technical skills, and though these may come naturally, they still have to work hard to refine and perfect them.

Technical factors refer to the individual skills required to perform a given task—and every objective an athlete wants to achieve will require a suite of technical skills that can deliver on the output for that performance, whether that is delivering a curling rock or driving a race car. In sport, technical factors can refer to broad categories, such as shooting, skating, running, attacking, or defending. They can also refer to very specific subcategories. Can a soccer player shoot the ball with both their dominant and non-dominant foot? Do they have the technical ability to strike the ball with different parts of their foot from different types of passes? Are they good at taking free kicks, or at curling the ball around a wall set up by defenders? Just like with the previous factors, the higher the level of competition, the more refined the suite of required technical components becomes. For an aspiring professional basketball player who wants to play point guard, the better their dribbling and passing skills, the more likely they are to progress to the next level.

There were numerous technical aspects to Finn's World Cup run that were obvious to any viewer, and numerous others that involved great mastery but likely seemed effortless. Riding over steep rocky terrain requires you to control the movement of the bike at precise moments. Similarly, maintaining a high level of control over your bike while you are jumping through the air or dropping off larger transitions can make it look graceful and smooth. So does carrying speed through tight corners while putting the bike at the right angle against the berm at the same time as you apply the exact right level of pressure to the brakes at the exact right moment.

Success in every discipline involves mastery of a specific set of technical factors. Are you a good public speaker, or do you engage well with the media? At work, do you have the skills to deal with IT demands (say, coding efficiently in the necessary language) or financial challenges (such as accurately forecasting the impacts of price changes on sales and revenue)? A musician would need to understand various techniques to produce sounds relative to their instrument (finger picking for guitar), just as a woodworker might acquire and refine their own set of skills (carving or finishing). If you regularly deal with people, do you have the adequate and appropriate communication skills?

EXAMPLES OF TECHNICAL FACTORS

Mountain biking: Body positioning over obstacles; cornering and balancing skills; pedal stroke efficiency

Ice hockey: Shooting; skating; passing; face-offs

Business: Negotiating; accounting; problem-solving; project management; IT proficiency; budget projecting

Music: Bowing; breath control; picking patterns; listening skills

Tactical Factors

Tactics relate to the way you choose to apply your skills, and how you approach the situations and challenges that are part of your performance. Consistently high performers know how to choose the right tactics at the right time. There are also many highly skilled athletes or executives who underperform—consistently or in a given event—because they make the wrong decisions in crucial moments. Those poor tactical choices limit the ability of their physical, mental, or technical skills to adequately influence their output.

Returning to Finn's World Cup race as an example, he applied several tactics in order to influence his output. Like every other rider in that race, he had studied each individual section on the course and had prepared a plan for how to ride each one, setting up his bike accordingly.

The more you investigate what determines the output, **the more you will see the importance of the Core 4 attributes in any performance.**

He and his team would have walked the course before the race to gather information; they would have watched the other riders during the training and qualifying runs to learn their approaches; and they would have studied the course again on the day of the race to assess the conditions. Finn and his teammates and coaches would have taken in as much information as possible to calculate the best strategy for producing the required output on that specific course on that specific day. At the moment Finn launched his run, his aggressive start helped him gain time early in the race—time he was able to use to influence his approach to later sections of the course. The lines he chose in each corner, jump, and technical section were different from the lines that other riders chose, and he and his team selected them to play into his unique strengths. When his chain broke, he instantly changed his tactic for the last part of the race so he could carry enough speed to hold onto his lead.

Tactics can impact performance at both the individual and team levels. In a team sport, tactics are often determined by the coach, who decides how the team may want to attack, defend, or play when on a powerplay. Tactics can change from game to game, or throughout a game. When a team plays on the road against a hostile crowd and an aggressive home team, the coach might direct them to play cautiously and defensively for the first ten to twenty minutes and let the facing team come at them with everything they have, and then to shift into an attacking strategy for the rest of the game once the other team has depleted some of their energy and the excitement has worn off. In a team sport, it's important that each player understands the tactical element of their individual role and is able to execute what is expected of them. When a less skilled team beats a favored opponent, it is often due to excellent tactical execution as a team. Conversely, a highly skilled team with poor tactics or team strategy can often disappoint its fans.

Tactics also play an important role in personal and professional environments. Lacking the tactics to handle challenging situations can lead to problems in personal relationships or business decisions. In an organization, do you have the tactical skill set to be a leader? Do you know how to approach problems that drive or challenge a corporation to target certain markets? What tactics are needed in relationships with various employees? As an investor, tactics guide what you invest in, the timing, and the different strategies you might use. For an entrepreneur, what are the tactics involved with pushing your own social media platform or driving self-promotion?

EXAMPLES OF TACTICAL FACTORS

MOUNTAIN BIKING: Race strategy (when to draft and when to attack); gear changing; use of brakes in cornering; line choice

ICE HOCKEY: Attacking strategy with teammates; how you play against specific players; penalty kill formation and positioning

BUSINESS: Pricing strategies; customer service and retention; cross promotion; product placement; use of technology; delegating; conflict resolution

MUSIC: Application of music theory; choice of songs for an album; how to distribute your music

How the Core 4 Relate to Output

All performances have physical, mental, technical, and tactical aspects. Of course, the output requirement of an elite athlete is very different from that of an executive or a musician; however, be it in sport, business, music, or life, every type of performance you do can be influenced by factors within the Core 4. Some of these categories might not seem to relate deeply to some performances (for example, on the surface it might seem like that highly skilled violin player I described in the introduction might have few tactical requirements to do her job—though she might disagree), but the more you investigate what determines the output, the more you will see the importance of the Core 4 attributes in any performance.

The relationship becomes easier to see when the output is required over longer periods of time or on an ongoing basis. Take for example a person who regularly works ten-hour shifts four days in a row in a hospital emergency room. There is little room for error over those four days; each decision and action could literally result in life or death, and when and for how long that person will be required to perform at a high level cannot be predicted. If you break down the output that a surgeon, nurse, or administrator requires in order to deliver a high performance, you can easily identify the physical, mental,

While each Core 4 attribute is a unique contributor to performance, they do not work independently of each other. **They can and do influence each other.**

technical, and tactical attributes that will affect that output. The surgeon and the nurse are on their feet all day—a physical factor. The surgeon needs a high level of technical skills to perform an operation; the nurse has to be able to insert a catheter or an IV; the administrator must be an excellent communicator and be adept at multiple software programs and IT systems. All three have to know how to conserve their energy for the intense bursts of activity that accompany a serious admittance like a car-crash survivor, and all three need to be able to focus when an admittance like that arrives suddenly at the end of their grueling shift.

If you can imagine what it would be like to perform on demand in that environment (or if you have direct experience), you can start to understand that while each Core 4 attribute is a unique contributor to performance, they do not work independently of each other. They can and do influence each other. This interaction is called *integration*, and it's what we'll be examining in the next chapter.

Lesson Learned

While there are thousands of factors related to high performance, they can all be categorized into four areas: physical, mental, technical, and tactical—the Core 4. Different outputs will require different levels of contribution in each performance factor, but all will play some kind of role. Recognizing this and understanding how the Core 4 will affect your output is foundational to your preparation for performance.

3

Understanding Integration

Just like the workings of an engine or a clock, the gears of performance function together to produce the output.

As a physiologist, I view my work through a systems approach to performance. Human physiology is the study of how the body works. There are a number of components within the discipline, including fields (like biology, physics, and chemistry) that work together to support how the body functions. In turn, physiology applies these many components and subcomponents to numerous systems: digestive, endocrine, reproductive, neuromuscular, cardiovascular, and pulmonary. These individual systems do not work in isolation from each other—they overlap in many ways. For example, the cardiovascular system works to deliver blood, while the pulmonary system controls the gas exchange within that blood, bringing in oxygen and getting rid of carbon dioxide. Both systems in turn work with the skeletal and muscular systems. Every time a human performs an act, like lifting a weight, these various systems will play a role either in the action itself, or in the body's response to that action.

A systems approach to physiology accounts for this type of interplay. Performance, too, requires a systems approach. In the previous chapter, I illustrated the Core 4 factors—physical, mental, technical, and tactical—by showing each in its own circle, sitting on its own. It was natural for me to present it in that way, just as it was natural for you to find that easy to understand. As humans, we like to compartmentalize information, so we can focus on processing a single area at a time. But while this perspective was helpful in explaining how each of the Core 4 factors influence your output in their own way, the reality is that they are highly integrated—each category interacts with and influences the other to produce an output, and no single factor can operate in a way that supports performance on its own. For that reason, appreciating integration is an important aspect of understanding performance as an output.

Generating an output requires input from all four areas, and each has a direct influence on the expression of the other three. For example, a snowboard cross racer with a high level of technical skills may be the fastest on the course through qualifying when they race by themselves, but they might struggle when racing in a heat

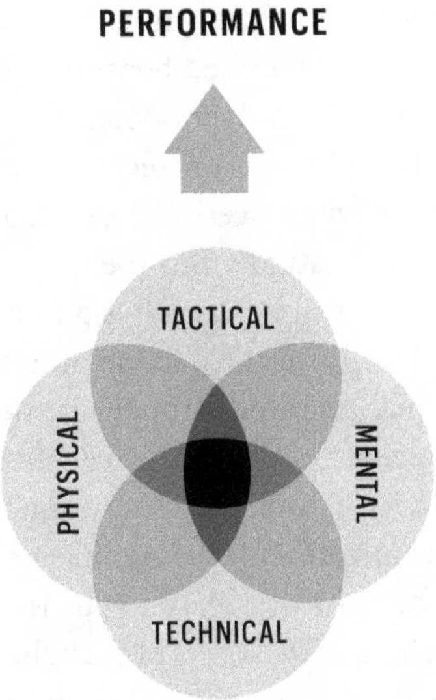

Performance as an Integrated Output of Your Core 4

because they don't have the tactical expertise of knowing when to pass or how to protect a lead by allowing that competitor to draft off them (a term for riding behind another rider to reduce wind resistance and preserve your energy or increase speed to pass). Similarly, they might not possess the mental skills to handle the pressure, or have the confidence in their skills when racing in close contact against other riders in a heat. A rider's lack of tactical and mental attributes might limit their ability to utilize their technical skill to ride at high speeds. Or a soccer player who has great technical skill but poor physical abilities may dominate early on in an intense match but be relatively ineffective, or even a liability, when they tire in the later parts of the game. Their ability to use their technical skills is limited because they can't get to the ball or get away from their opponent.

The impact of physical on technical and tactical is usually the most obvious overlap—especially in cases like that soccer player's fatigue. But the impact of the mental on the physical can be equally significant. In a solo cycling time trial, it is critical for an athlete to mentally focus on producing power through the pedals to maintain maximal speed. They call this trial "the race of truth," as each athlete is on their own and cannot draft off an opponent or teammate. It takes significant mental effort to block out the pain you feel in your legs, lungs, and body when pushing at the limits of your ability for twenty minutes or more. In a race like this, any lapse in mental focus will negatively impact your ability to express your true physical capabilities.

The Gears of Performance

One approach I like to use when working with clients is to present the Core 4 as big "gears" that drive performance. Just like the workings of an engine or a clock, the gears of performance function together to produce the output.

This idea comes from Dr. Howie Wenger, the University of Victoria physiology professor (and personal mentor) whom I told you about in the introduction to this book. I first came across Dr. Wenger's "gear" concept in

1996, and since then I have seen many experts and practitioners expand on this model and modify it for different needs and different sports. But in each case, the fundamental structure always remains unchanged: none of the Core 4 aspects of performance can be separated from the others, and any change in one will affect all of the others, just like with a set of interlocking gears.

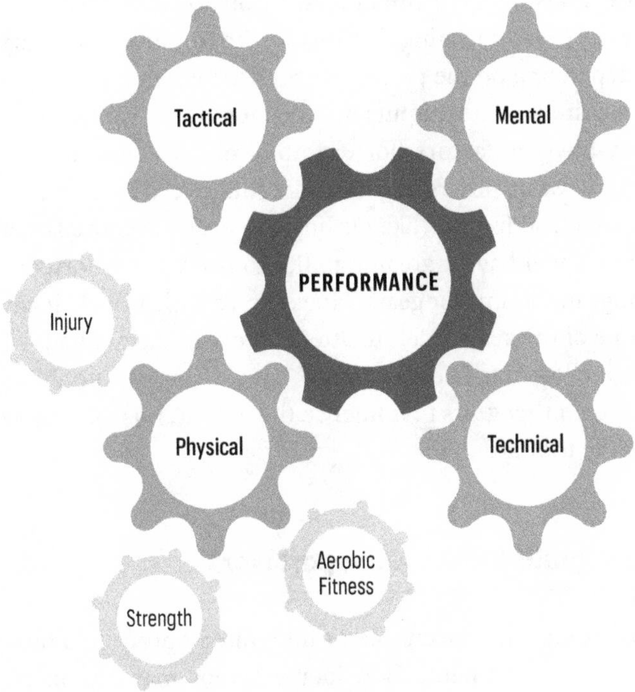

The Gears of Performance

Learning this invaluable gear analogy early in my career was a major influence in shaping my perspective on performance to what it is today. This model can be used for any kind of performance. Optimal performance sits at the middle, and each of the Core 4 gears must be moving effectively and efficiently to turn it. All of the factors are integrated, and that integration occurs on a continuum—each gear is unique in its size and role, but it still cannot be separated from the whole, and each depends on all of the others. Meanwhile, the "size" of each gear—meaning, it's relative importance—will vary depending on the performance objective and the output required. Some outputs may be more heavily influenced by physical factors (for example, middle-distance running) while others may be more influenced by technical or tactical factors (like curling). In each case, the larger gears will have a greater ability to overcome shortcomings in the smaller gears. However, as with a clock, if any one of the gears is left unattended or not maintained—if it is allowed to become "rusty"—it will impede the ability of the other gears to influence the output, no matter how large they are.

Integration in the Non-sport World

Let's look at an example of integrated output in a business environment. Consider a senior manager in an accounting firm—let's call her Susan—who works with the company's largest clients. Susan has considerable tax accounting expertise (technical) that is a valued asset to both the company and its clients. She is capable of analyzing various scenarios quickly and sees opportunities and threats that others don't, so she is often brought in to advise on complex deals and to convince clients to work with her firm. She can deliver solutions in high-pressure situations with millions of dollars on the line, on demand (mental). Challenging accounting problems that may take other members of the department several days to work through, Susan can solve in a single meeting. She is also capable of "reading the room" and understanding each client's perspective, and she varies her delivery and approach when conveying information about the solution her team has chosen (tactical). She isn't particularly physically active but she regularly goes for walks with her family, and that keeps her feeling energized, healthy, and ready to go to work (physical). Susan's bosses and officemates refer to her as their MVP—their most valuable player. She is a high performer, and that's what separates her firm from several local competitors. When people describe Susan, they refer to her as an expert in the technical and tactical areas of her work and someone who can perform under pressure.

After a few years of watching Susan deliver high performances for local clients, the company wants to expand her impact to their clients across the country. At first, Susan's bosses send her out on a trip every one to two months. The results are impressive and everyone is happy. Word gets out about how good Susan is, and the demands on her time and focus increase, leading to more

Each "gear" is unique in its size and role, but it still cannot be separated from the whole, **and each depends on all of the others.**

trips and more clients. After a year, the solutions aren't coming as easily to Susan, and although her work is still well above what the other accountants are providing, her performance starts to drop off ever so slightly. She is starting to feel a bit run down with all the travel, and she finds she is getting colds and sniffles a little more often. She also starts to notice the impact of her new role on her overall energy going into meetings and on her ability to tolerate little things that never used to bother her, including clients wanting her to explain her solutions. These issues don't seem to impact the output, but Susan finds herself thinking about them after meetings more than ever before. She is also starting to worry about her youngest child at home, who is experiencing some separation anxiety. Susan is still a high performer, and everyone is still happy with her results, but she is beginning to question how long she can keep it up.

Before Susan's work expanded across the country, she had been demonstrating significant capacity to perform on demand. You could argue that she had sufficient capacity in each of the gears to deliver the output, though clearly technical was the largest gear, and overwhelmingly drove her performance. If you were to draw a gear chart, the mental and tactical gears would likely be moderately sized, as Susan's work requires both factors and she possesses all the skills required for each. Physical would likely be a very small gear, as delivering in a local environment a couple of times a week requires very little physical output, other than being present.

However, as the demands on her time begin to pick up—as she is asked to do more travel and handle more clients—Susan's ability to deliver on demand has started to diminish.

Why would this happen? The challenges she is facing now aren't any more complex, and the client perspectives and personalities don't require new approaches in delivery. And Susan's technical and tactical skill sets are still the best in her company. Still, her performance is starting to deteriorate—because as the performance environment changed, so did the required output for each of the Core 4. No longer can Susan deliver solutions to clients in her own hometown. Now she has to deliver solutions in an unfamiliar environment, after sleeping in a hotel and waiting in an airport, eating less healthy foods and sometimes changing time zones. The physical attributes needed to produce the new required output have increased. While her moderately sized physical gear had been sufficient for the occasional trip early on, it has become inadequate as the demands change. The new output simply has a greater physical requirement than Susan's capacity, which is why she is starting to become fatigued.

This issue is further compounded by a reduction in Susan's capacity: with the increased demand on her time, she is doing less walking, and all the eating in restaurants has led to some weight gain. At the same time, the fatigue is leading Susan to become more irritable with clients, and she is finding herself mentally distracted and feeling the pressure of decision-making more intently. The requirement for mental skills in client meetings hasn't changed, nor has her skill sets, but the additional stress, both from her work and at home, is undermining the functioning of her mental gear. Susan's ability to deliver the output with her key technical and tactical gears has become influenced by both her physical and mental gears. Most of us know already that people can't perform at the same level when they are tired. Every athlete experiences days when they just don't have it: they feel fatigued, or unfocused, or unmotivated. If you are a parent, you definitely know that when your kids haven't eaten or slept, they do not function well. The challenge is being able to fully appreciate how this knowledge applies to performance, and to think in an integrated manner every time we are analyzing and planning a required output.

You can clearly see the importance of integration when you begin to understand that performance in any field is dependent on first ensuring you have a basic level of physical and mental health. It goes without saying that if you are sick, injured, have a disease, or are mentally unwell, you may not be able to perform at all, let alone at a high level.

The integrated nature of performance is a well-known fact in high-performance sport, yet even those of us who live and work in this field—including managers, coaches, practitioners, and athletes—are constantly struggling to put that knowledge into action. Many teams have distinct specialists to support performance in each of the Core 4 factors. But providing separate support for those four areas is not integration. We all have our biases and areas of comfort, so each of us will tend to view performance through a particular lens, and give more weight to a particular gear. Integrating is an action, and it needs to be done intentionally.

Just like with our accountant Susan, you and every other human will perform at a level that's a product of your physical, mental, technical, and tactical attributes, and as each of those attributes change—in importance or in ability—they will affect all of the others. It is important that you view your performance from an integrated perspective and clearly articulate the actual output that's required to achieve your performance objective. It is equally important to understand integration so that you optimally prepare yourself for sustainable performance.

Lesson Learned

Each of the Core 4 factors interacts with and influences the other in a highly integrated way to produce an output. No single factor can operate in a way that supports performance on its own. The Core 4 can be viewed as big "gears" of performance, and, just like the workings of an engine or a clock, they function together to produce the output.

PART 2

BECOMING A HIGH PERFORMER

4

Developing the Qualities of a High Performer

Performance can be simplified, but that doesn't mean it's easy.

WHEN WE see an athlete win an Olympic medal or a most valuable player award, our natural reaction is to think that they are so good at what they do. We are in awe at the level and precision of their delivery, and we believe there is something special about them, something that sets them apart from the rest of us. We think these high performers must have a natural capacity to deliver an integrated output that is at or above the level required to achieve their objective, and to do it on demand, consistently.

But what we see on TV or from the stands is only the finished product. We don't see the work that goes into it: the slow progressive steps they took over years to develop their ability to perform. As they progressed through their careers, these athletes were slowly improving their ability to produce that output and refine their craft. If they are a high performer now, at the elite level, they may have also been a high performer when they were at the lower levels, even while they were still developing their ability to produce the output that you see now. They were delivering the necessary and expected output at the junior level back then, just as they deliver the necessary and expected output at the elite level today. But there are also many people who weren't high performers earlier in their careers. They may have had the "potential" to be, but were lacking in certain areas. They had to learn to be a high performer along the way—to work and develop the character traits that allow them to perform on demand at the highest level. Many athletes have had to learn to be disciplined, to perform under pressure, to be purposeful in their actions, or to take ownership of their own performance. For many, these traits don't come naturally. But they can be developed.

What Does It Mean to Be a High Performer?

So, when we talk about high performers, who exactly do we mean? Is it the person who constantly competes for the top position in race after race? Is it the person who regularly wins those individual awards or championships?

Or is it the rainmaker executive who lands every contract they go after? It is and can be all of these, yes—but, depending on the individual and their goals, high performance can also be far more complex than this, and far less easy to measure. Remember what I said at the start of this book: performance refers to the *output*: the action of carrying out a task or function. It is about how well an individual or a team can execute what they are trying to do to create the required output. A high performer is anyone who does this at a high level, on demand.

In sport, there is a common assumption that when we speak about high performers, we are speaking of those athletes who produce higher outputs than their competition. Many times this is true, especially when that output is what is required to win. But that assumption can lead many people to believe that high performance is something out of their reach, reserved only for the "best of the best." And while there will always be the top 1 or 2 percent of performers in any sport, business, art, or activity, there is plenty of space for everyone to become a high performer. In almost every Olympic Games, there has been that one underdog athlete who finished in the top ten, or even the top five, when no one expected them to be even close to the top twenty. There have also been many athletes who reached a personal best on demand and on the biggest stage but finished far from the podium, in the fifth, twelfth, or even eighteenth place. Similarly, there have been many, many times when a high performer who was expected to take gold did not grab a medal at all—something out of their control affected the outcome.

In my experience, people who are in pursuit of high performance often fall into one of four categories:

1. An individual whose objective is to be their personal best and they can consistently deliver on that output, and being their personal best also aligns with being the best in their field of choice. This is a high performer.
2. An individual whose objective is to be their personal best and they can consistently deliver on that output, but being their personal best does *not* align with being the best in their field of choice. This is also a high performer.
3. An individual whose objective is to be their personal best, and this aligns with being the best in their field, but they cannot consistently deliver. This is not a high performer.
4. An individual whose objective is to be their personal best, and this does *not* align with being the best in their field, but they still cannot consistently deliver. This is also not a high performer.

There are so many people in a wide range of fields who are producing great performances relative to the output that is required for their personal objective. Most importantly, they are producing outputs that are at or above their personal expectations. What you need to understand is that this can include *anyone* in the field, not just the top performers. Anyone who

To be a high performer, you *must* be willing to **own your own performance.**

is achieving performance at or above their own expectations on demand is optimizing their output. They are high performers. This means that you cannot and should not judge your own performance on other people's expectation of what high performance is, unless those expectations align with the output required for your objective.

An athlete who wins gold at the Olympics is a high performer if they delivered the required output on demand. So is an athlete who was not expected to make it to the Olympics at all but did, and who finished in the top ten.

For purposes of this book, when I speak about high performers, I am speaking about all individuals and teams who optimize their performance on demand, not just "the best of the best."

Can Anyone Be a High Performer?

The simplest answer to this is yes—everyone is capable of preparing themselves to accomplish a given task or function if it is realistically within their potential. Of course, whether or not a person fulfills that potential in a given moment will depend on the goals and objectives, and the output that is required to achieve them. Sometimes, when the goals are clear and the potential is there, it just doesn't happen. It might be a lack of opportunity, or a lack of awareness, or sometimes it's a disconnect between a person's expectations and the reality of the level of work that is needed. Performance can be simplified, but that doesn't mean it's easy. Some people are just not committed to doing the work. Others believe that wanting to be at the next level is enough to get them there. Over the years, in environments ranging from high school to Olympic-level sport, I have worked with many athletes who have set high expectations for the level they want to achieve, and who truly believe they want to make it to college, become a professional, or go to the Olympics, but who still end up skipping workouts, taking long breaks, or relying only on skill while failing to address the physical gaps they need to overcome to move forward. Others fail to put in the work it takes to truly understand the required output, and so have unrealistic expectations about their own capacities and what it will take to succeed.

What Sets High Performers Apart?

High performers want to be at their best, consistently. The high performers I have met in my career are people who seek out optimal performance both personally and professionally, whether they are in sport, business, or any other field.

The most successful athletes I have worked with are always connected to a true passion for what they are doing. More than that, they want to be the best they can be at their sport. This doesn't always mean the best at their sport. I have also met many athletes who are not interested in giving a 100-percent effort to their sport, and who don't care about being the best they can be. As a fan, these are the athletes that can frustrate you with flashes of brilliance but no consistency. They may still be good athletes, and they can be perfectly comfortable doing what they need to do to get by. But they are not consistent high performers.

In my long experience working with high performers in sport and business, I consistently see certain characteristics appear again and again, no matter what field they are performing in:

1. They have a growth mindset.
2. They are competitive.
3. They are focused, disciplined, and willing to do the work.
4. They control what they can control.
5. They are strategic in their approach.
6. They put themselves in a culture that supports high performance.
7. They set clear objectives and are purposeful in what they do.
8. They understand that preparation is key.

We'll talk about the last two characteristics in later chapters; for now, let's dive a little further into each of the first six.

They Have a Growth Mindset

The concept of mindset has gained popular appeal in recent years, and there are many books about how it can boost performance. In her book *Mindset: The New Psychology of Success*, Dr. Carol Dweck expertly articulates two mindsets that have a powerful effect on our ability to achieve: *fixed* and *growth*. According to Dr. Dweck, a person with a fixed mindset believes their qualities and characteristics are not likely to change. They assume that "they are what they are," and they have to do the best they can with what they've got. A person with a growth mindset, on the other hand, believes they have the ability to improve in a given area if they make the effort. They assume that, whatever their abilities or natural tendencies are now, they can change and learn if they want to.

The athletes and executives I have met who succeed at reaching their objective and achieving their optimal performance typically have a growth mindset. They seek out things that can help them to be the best they can be. Whatever their current level—elite, developing, just starting out—they don't want to just get by. A few years ago, I was working with an experienced professional athlete, and I could see immediately that he understood how different performance factors were directly and indirectly impacting his performance on and off the court. But despite his talent, he didn't just assume he knew everything: even later in his career, after he had already won *two* MVP awards, he was still willing to learn. At every stage and skill level, he was curious, he paid attention to details, and he asked a lot of questions. He had a desire to

High performers
don't just set goals and
then build out a plan
to achieve them—
they *do* achieve them.

be better and more efficient with his efforts, and he was open to learning new ways to make that happen, and to sustain that continuous improvement over the long term. He had a growth mindset.

They Are Competitive

This is a simple, hard truth: to be a high performer, you *must* be willing to own your own performance. In today's culture, we are often discouraged from being competitive, and the idea of wanting to outperform others has taken on somewhat of a negative connotation. Parents, school systems, sports programs, and even society at large have been intentionally and unintentionally removing competition from our daily lives. It's beyond the scope of this book to debate whether this is right or wrong, but I will say that, in my experience, *all* high performers are competitive.

But here is an important distinction: I am not saying that all competitive people are high performers. Like with many qualities, being competitive has its negative side. It can be misunderstood, and it can be misguided. When it results in cheating, poor behavior, harm to others, or the total neglect of other important parts of your life, competitiveness is neither healthy nor ethical. Being overly competitive in inappropriate situations or becoming obsessed with things you have no control over can lead to mistakes, disappointment, and mental health challenges—none of which promote sustainable high performance.

All of that said, if you are going to improve and push your current limits, you have to challenge yourself. There is such a thing as healthy competition, and it is both internally and externally driven. High performers find competition within themselves, and against others. And, most importantly, they are competitive in a way that is focused on *output*.

They Are Focused, Disciplined, and Willing to Do the Work

High performers express their passion by showing persistence, discipline, and commitment. They're willing to work hard, and they do whatever it takes to get where they want to go. High performers don't just set goals and then build out a plan to achieve them—they *do* achieve them.

I mentioned earlier that high performance isn't easy. As you work to improve your Core 4 profile (which we'll talk more about in Chapter 6) and your ability to deliver the necessary output, you are going to come up against times that are difficult. In my career, I have often seen both athletes and executives get sidetracked on one stumbling block in particular: the progress they need to make requires an intermediary step that they don't like to do, or that doesn't come naturally to them. The high performers are the ones that don't get distracted by the fact that they don't enjoy doing something, or that they'd rather be doing something else. They stay focused and disciplined on doing what they need to do to improve their output.

Take, for example, someone who wants to increase their physical capacity to handle work. To do this, you have to work hard at aerobic activity, either at or near your current capacity. The progress is physically and mentally taxing, and it doesn't happen overnight. When you do see progress, it is gradual, and you have to put more regular effort in just to maintain it. For a high-performing executive who has a busy travel schedule, prioritizing the time to fit in that training requires commitment and discipline. They remain focused on their objectives, and that allows them to get up early before work to do their workouts.

For many high performers, this type of preparation becomes habitual. (James Clear does a great job of explaining different ways to develop this kind of practice in his book *Atomic Habits*.) They create a habit of doing the little things every day to make sure they are prepared when they need to perform. Even when they are on the road or have other stressors in their life, they do not let those distractions disrupt their habits or take their focus away from their objectives. High performers are willing to put in the hard work even when part of them doesn't want to.

They Control What They Can Control

High performers realize that they're in control of their own performance. They accept and take responsibility for all that they do. By doing this, they gain the ability to set and meet goals.

Serial high performers focus their efforts on the things that they can influence and don't waste time worrying about the things that they can't. An athlete might not have any control over when a competition will be scheduled, for example, but they do have control over how they plan around that schedule. So that is where they put in the work, optimizing their training and preparation around that date. Another thing an athlete does not have control over is who they will be performing against—who those athletes are, how they prepare, what level of talent they have. But they do have control over their own preparation, over their own ability to study that opposition, and over how they plan to compete against them.

This same focus on what the athlete can control persists during competition. High performers realize that they don't have control over what another athlete does during a race or what calls the referees will make, but they do have control over how they respond to these obstacles. They don't let themselves get distracted by things that are out of their control, which allows them to direct their efforts toward delivering the output required.

At a competition I once attended, I watched a young coach speak to a veteran athlete about what was happening with one of the competitors. While the coach's intentions were good—he was sharing the information to help inform the athlete of the current situation—the veteran got upset and shut him out. Later that night I spoke with the athlete about what had happened, and he explained that the information would have given him no benefit in the moment. It was just a distraction, and he needed to keep his priorities straight. "I had no control over what the other athlete did," he told me. "It wasn't what he said, it was that he presented it to me in a way that risked taking my focus away from what I needed to do."

They Are Strategic in Their Approach

Strategy is the big picture; it is everything put together. The word strategy is often used interchangeably with tactics, but when I refer to strategy, I'm talking about the combination of everything you're trying to do to prepare for your performance objective. Tactics, in the context of this book, refers only to the decisions and strategies you use in the actual field of play to influence the output.

When I say that consistent high performers are strategic in their approach, I don't mean that they always follow intricately detailed plans or that they all have extensive teams of support. What they do typically have is very clear objectives. On top of that, they understand the outputs required to achieve those objectives, and they prepare themselves to deliver those outputs. They pay attention to the most important aspects of their objective and what it will take to achieve that objective. Elite athletes and successful professionals view performance from an output perspective, not from an outcome perspective. They identify the key metrics that are associated with the specific output that is required, and then they evaluate their progress against those metrics. They establish a clear direction as to how they are going to prepare themselves, and this direction guides all of their decision-making along the way. They ensure that any efforts they put forth are purposeful in terms of achieving their objective. If it will have a minimal impact, they will avoid wasting effort on it.

They Are in a Culture That Supports High Performance

Strategy is nothing without the right culture surrounding it. A colleague and mentor of mine once said that culture kicks the s—t out of strategy every day, and I couldn't agree with him more. A strong culture can pull an okay strategy along with it and make it successful, but a great strategy will be blown apart by a bad culture.

Serial high performers can only thrive in a culture that supports high performance, whether that is a team of two people or a squad of fifty-plus. In an organization with a toxic or non-supportive culture, high performers will create their own, insulating themselves from the larger team and surrounding themselves with whomever they can find who can help them to be their best. They literally create their own cultural bubble within or alongside the larger organization. And if they can't find that bubble? They leave.

Remember what I said in Part I about integration? Integration plays an equally important role in how a high performer responds to culture (and, in fact, it plays an important role in all of the characteristics in this list). The reason a high performer will not stay in a poor culture is *because* of their growth mindset, *because* they are competitive, *because* they will control whatever they can control. If they cannot find a solution to the lack of support they are experiencing, they will move on from it in order to achieve or maintain sustainable high performance. That means it is crucial for leaders to take responsibility for the culture that exists within their environment and ensure alignment between their organization's objective,

Strategy is nothing
without the right
culture surrounding it.

culture, and actions. As a leader, your most important job is to set a culture that will facilitate high performance.

Do All High Performers Have All of These Traits?

High performers have the capacity for these traits, and most of them can be learned. However, they may not have all of these traits all the time, or in all aspects of their life. A small percentage of the high performers I have worked with do demonstrate all of these traits, all of the time. But the vast majority are simply capable of demonstrating the necessary traits at the moment they are needed.

For example, an athlete or executive may have a growth mindset when it comes to their ability to learn technical skills, but more of a fixed mindset around certain physical qualities. Even highly accomplished people who have come to me for help with improving their performance will often make comments like, "It's just who I am," or, "My body doesn't respond to that type of training," or, "I don't have the time to do that." They want to learn to be better and they believe they can change some things, but when it comes to other areas, they suddenly have a fixed mindset. We often think of athletes as knowing exactly what they want to do and what sport they want to play right from their earliest ages. But this is not always the case. Sometimes an athlete enters a sport reluctantly but ends up loving it. And sometimes a professional suddenly has to change their role or even change their field, and they find a new passion they didn't know existed.

Within any team environment, there are going to be people who are very good at what they do but who don't really care about being the best they can be. In sports, you will find players who care about being an athlete—about reaching some level of success and living an athlete's lifestyle—but they don't need more than that. Often, these athletes are either incredibly gifted, talent-wise, and they get by in spite of their low level of effort, or they play in a sport that does not have a lot of competition and they can be successful at a high level due to the lack of depth of field. And for them, that's just fine. For others, and maybe for you, it's not enough.

It's important to repeat that many of the high performers I've worked with and observed weren't born with all of these traits. Certainly, some had many high-performance characteristics that were innate from birth, and some developed them through the environment they grew up in. But countless high performers across countless fields have had to work their whole careers to intentionally develop these traits. To varying degrees, every one of these eight characteristics can be learned and sustained. The ability to understand this fact, and to embrace the effort required, is the first step in becoming a high performer.

Lesson Learned

Yes, there are specific personal qualities that define a high performer, but those qualities can be learned. Having a growth mindset, wanting to win and doing the work to get there, focusing on what you can control, being strategic and purposeful, and seeking out the culture that can support you in your objectives can all help you reach those objectives in every area of your life.

5

Setting Your Performance Objective

Understanding your "why" is a key first step in clarifying your performance objectives.

WHEN I work with athletes, coaches, and organizations on performance strategy, I spend a fair amount of time helping them set clear performance objectives. Your performance objectives define the targets that will determine the required output, so I cannot overstate their importance.

So, what is a performance objective? Simply put, it is the main thing you want to achieve. They can be individual, or for the team. In sport, a performance objective would usually be winning a race or a championship, becoming MVP, or achieving a certain level of competition. What drives a person to achieve these objectives will be different for each individual. Some will relate it to their identity; some will see it as a path to fame or money. Others may only want to be the best they can be at what they do.

Throughout this book, I have been telling you stories about a wide range of athletes and corporate professionals who achieved their own version of success. What that success looks like varies from story to story, but one success is not better than any other. They are specific to the individual. The people in these stories have been willing to make their own type of sacrifices, and each has their own natural strengths to leverage and weaknesses to improve. Their objectives and priorities are different, so they measure their output and performance differently. To me, the story of an athlete winning Olympic gold is no more or less inspiring than that of an executive who builds a billion-dollar company while performing at a high level as a parent—or a manager who wants to improve their health while going back to school, or an athlete who strives to be their best while having the chance to play at the collegiate level. Yes, some may be more difficult to achieve than others, or may require a higher level of output in a specific area, but performance objectives are personal and are specific to every individual or team. They are also dynamic—they change over time.

Defining Your Performance Objectives

Remember that when I speak about optimizing your performance, I'm referring to how well you perform your tasks to achieve a specific objective. Naturally, then, it follows that you first need to define that specific objective—only then can you determine what your performance output actually needs to be.

Your performance objective is strictly personal and should be 100-percent related to you. If it's not, you'll have a difficult time achieving and sustaining a high level of performance. Take the time to think about how you want to define performance for yourself. Is it hitting a certain level or milestone on a certain day? Over the course of a year, or five years? Does it have multiple components to it? Is your performance very specific, or is it multifaceted?

If you don't have objectives and don't know what you're planning for or trying to achieve, then you are doing unprepared guesswork—you are "winging it." The more specific you can be, the better you can understand the required output, and the more effective your planning can be: it can be a narrow objective, like riding a particular time in a particular road race, or it can be broader, like staying fit and able to compete through your fifties. Maybe it's a set sales total for the next twelve months, or to reach a certain level at your company within three years, or to complete a six-week training program that will prepare you to lead an upcoming project. Perhaps your aspiration is to win an event at the Olympics in four years. Whatever your objective is, you need to define it clearly.

In team environments, performance objectives get a bit more complex. They still need to be personal and clear, but also framed in the context of the team's objective.

What is your role, and what output do you need to deliver to help the team achieve its goal? It is important that you try not to create a situation in which your personal objective competes with your team's objective—that dynamic is very likely to end in failure. You see this regularly in sport, when some athletes on a team are playing for themselves, trying to pad their personal stats to get their next contract, or when they disagree with the coach on how they can best help the team while neglecting the role that is critical to their team's success. Their personal objective is not aligned with what the team needs, and the result is a disconnected team that will likely underachieve based on their talent.

Understanding Your Why

One of the key lessons I've learned while working with high performers is the importance of deeply understanding the *why*. Coaches, practitioners, and athletes use many different approaches—from purpose maps and vision boards to priority weighting and mission statements—to help identify their why. These approaches typically revolve around the same two central questions: "Why do you do what you do?" and "Why do you want to achieve your objective?"

It seems so simple, but these questions often don't get the attention they deserve, in sport or in any other field. Sure, you will hear coaches and executive teams talking about the general concept, but only rarely do I see a team or organization invest the full time they truly need to not only fully articulate the answers, but also to clearly communicate those answers to everyone involved.

The *why* is a key piece of what sets high performers apart. Most of the sustained high performers I've had the honor of working with are very clear in their why, and in what drives them to be successful. Over the years, I have witnessed a distinct relationship between a person's ability to understand why they are doing what they do and their ability to perform on demand. Meanwhile, those who have struggled with their why—or who weren't at the very least subconsciously connected to it—may have found some level of success, but they have rarely achieved sustained high performance.

When I first begin working with an athlete on setting their performance objectives, one of the first questions I ask is this: "Why are you competing in this sport?" Most of the time, I get one of two responses—either an immediate "I don't know" or an immediate "Because I love it!" This is where I find it important to dig down a little deeper with those athletes before we go any further.

A highly regarded junior national tennis player who was struggling with injuries and progression once came to me for help. She had been putting in lots of work, traveling around competing and trying to get points to increase her ranking, but she was feeling frustrated over the fact that, despite all this effort, she kept getting sidelined by injuries. She had once been a national champion, but now she felt like she was struggling with the pressure and losing ground in her progression. She told me that

Whatever your objective is, **you need to define it clearly.**

she was starting to question if her dream of playing at the college and professional levels was ever going to happen. She loved the sport and she still had goals, but she was beginning to wonder what she was doing.

As I listened to her explain all of this to me, I could clearly see that she had lost alignment with her why. She had lost track of what it was that got her into competitive sport in the first place. She was focusing on other people's expectations—and while these do sometimes need to be considered in certain contexts, they should never drive the process.

When she was finished telling me her story, I asked that key question: "Why do you play tennis?"

Her answer was straightforward and simple: "Because I love the sport."

That's when I delved deeper. *Why* did she love the sport? What did she love about it? Was it tennis specifically, or sport in general? If it was tennis, why wasn't she playing recreationally rather than putting in the time to train eight to ten times every week?

She thought about it, and then told me that she loved challenging herself, and that tennis was a sport in which she could find the right balance between success, challenge, and the belief that she can excel. She also had an internal drive to compete.

That was a proper "why." It's not enough to stop at "I love my job" or "I want to win." What is it about winning that you enjoy? Is it the recognition and accolades? The sense of self-accomplishment? The confirmation that no one else is better than you? When I ask people why they do what they do, they will often give me the answer they think they're supposed to give, or the answer they think I want to hear. What I want is to see them dig deep into their own motivations so they can truly understand their why.

It's so easy for us to get lost in the habit of doing the work or the training without ever going back to ask why we are doing it. If this feels familiar to you, that's okay. It doesn't mean that you don't love your career or your particular pursuit—you probably do. But what is it that you love about it? Do you love competition? Being recognized within your field? The feeling of winning, or making the sale, or solving the problem? Is it teamwork? Helping others? Having an impact on the world? The challenge of training, or of increasing your skills? What is the special spark that drives you?

Understanding your "why" is a key first step in clarifying your performance objectives. Whatever it is you do in your life, go back to why you are doing it in the first place. Then, drill down and ask further questions. What are you trying to achieve? What does success look like for you? From there, ask questions that seek to understand how your why connects with what you're trying to accomplish. Why do you want that as your objective? If it helps, write your answer down or try to explain it out loud to someone else.

I encourage you to not just think hard about this question, but also to ask it repeatedly. Ask why, and then ask why again. Each time you ask, think about yourself. Then think about everything. Family. Career. Sport. Your creative pursuits. Ask yourself why you do what you do in each environment: work, play, home. What do you like about each part of your life? What do you dislike? Why do you want to learn more about performance optimization? Why are you reading this book? Be honest with your answers.

Spend the time early on to try to clarify your reasons, because when you have to get up at five in the morning to catch a flight or you are finding yourself staying late at work for days on end, there's going to come a time when it starts to get tiring. Disappointment is related to expectations. You need to connect with why you are doing something. If what you're doing doesn't connect with your why, then your performance objectives may not be aligned with your true motivations.

For that junior national tennis player, once she was able to articulate why she played tennis at a competitive level, that knowledge helped her connect that motivation with her objective. More importantly, it helped her see how every part of what she was doing was or wasn't related to either her why or her objective. She was still a great player, but she had become caught up in the doing, and so was underperforming, growing frustrated with her game, and losing her sense of enjoyment for her time on the court and her time in training. But by articulating her why clearly to herself and then aligning that why with her objective, she was able to formulate and prioritize what was required of her to deliver the output to achieve that objective.

As a result of this work, she started to waste less time on chasing points and playing matches when she was unprepared. She focused on preparing her body to handle the travel and the training and to deliver the necessary output: competitive games. Everything she did to prepare now had a purpose that was directly connected to her why and her objective. She restructured her schedule, competing less and preparing more so she was able to play injury free. Those changes increased the quality of her training and her confidence on the court, and, ultimately, her output. She started winning matches again, which in turn positively reinforced her why. She went on to win the national championship for a second time and fulfilled her objective of playing college tennis on a scholarship. Of course, the road wasn't completely smooth—she encountered many bumps along the way—but having the ability to connect with her why acted as an anchor to refocus her commitment to the game and to continue to prepare for her objective with purpose.

Your objective and personal why will be different from someone else's. It may be focused and well thought out, making it simple to prioritize your goals and efforts. However, that doesn't mean you shouldn't ask more questions. You may find that your answers are broad and clear, or are things that you've always been aware of at some level. Perhaps you'll discover that your why is that you like to build and challenge yourself, or perhaps it's as simple as you love what you do. It starts with questions that might seem obvious but will be more challenging than you think. Ask yourself things like:

- Why do I love what I do—what is it that I love about it?
- Why do I want to do this?
- Why do I need to get to my objective?
- Why am I participating in this specific sport/career/field of study/company?
- What do I want to get out of my involvement?

When I ask consistent high performers these same questions, what I regularly see is that they have ready answers. They understand what they are trying to achieve and why it's important to them. But even if you're already there, you can always go further. Keep asking deeper questions, and keep expanding on your answers. For example, if your answer to "Why do I want to do this?" is that you want to challenge yourself, ask yourself questions such as:

- What does it mean to challenge myself?
- Do I want to be better than other people? Or the best I can be?
- What is the specific challenge that I want to face? Is it living up to an expectation that has been set for me? Is it balancing my business with my family?

Dive in. Get specific. Find the underlying reasons for *why* what you do is important to you.

Why Your "Why" Matters

As I have said many times to many clients, high performance isn't easy. Every high performer has to make sacrifices. If you are no longer able to experience your why, you will find that your ability to tolerate those sacrifices will start to diminish. Picture an athlete who plays at a high level in a particular league or with a particular team because they love the fluidity that culture allows and how it enables them to create within their sport. Now put them in an environment that is more rigid and structured and less free flowing. You can guess what happens: their performance suffers. Now imagine an aging athlete who wants to extend their career and continue to play at a high level. To support that goal, they put in hard hours of training to keep their physical attributes at the level required to deliver their output. For many people, this training would be tedious. But this athlete knows that the training will have a positive impact on minimizing injuries, allowing them to continue to enjoy the sport they love while competing against the best in the game. That knowledge makes them capable of putting in those early mornings and pushing through those tough drill routines—but take that why away and it would be a lot harder for them to find the motivation. The gym is still there, the training program is still there, but once the athlete no longer sees that positive impact that's connected to their why, they'll be far less likely to do it. Knowing your why allows you to better align your actions to your goals.

We all have a limited capacity.

Yes, you can increase it, but it will never be infinite, and some glasses will have to remain unfilled.

And this equation doesn't just apply to elite athletes. Say you're an executive who is physically active, and you love to challenge yourself. You decide to join a group of friends who are entering a high-level cycling event that's taking place at the end of the year. You have an objective: you want to be social and as competitive as you can be with your peers, while at the same time maintaining your family relationships and effectively supporting your business. At the start of your training, you have a detailed and challenging training routine lined up, and you even have access to an elite cycling coach. But while those strategies can maximize your physical capacity to ride in a short period of time, they do not take your current situation into account and may not have a net positive impact on your overall goal. You find yourself grinding through the workouts on your own, following your coach's rigid plan of extremely hard, high-intensity training sessions. It is an excellent regimen for training adaptation, but it is producing a lot of physical and mental fatigue, and that begins to spill over into both your personal and professional life. Soon, the sessions are depleting your reserves and forcing to you to spend time recovering that you would normally spend playing with your kids. You are putting in the work, but you are missing on your objective. One of two things is going to happen: you will either fall off your training program, or you will fail to optimize your performance in your overall objective—and by that I mean more than your cycling performance.

Some people are very clear in their choices—they know exactly why they do what they do. In my work, I find it fairly easy to help individuals who understand their why to achieve their goals. Often, it is simply a matter of reviewing their programming and plans and making a few tweaks to help them get more out of what they are currently doing. Other times, it's about managing moderators (travel schedules and environments) or unanticipated circumstances (injuries) that can cloud one's perspective on their why. But even athletes and professionals like this can get busy doing other things and lose track of their why in the process. Remember, your why is dynamic, and it will change. Or you may still know your why but find yourself struggling to figure out what's most important or how to produce meaningful results. You may feel a bit lost and not where you want to be at a given stage. That's when it's time to start prioritizing.

Which Glasses Are You Going to Fill?

I want to borrow yet another concept from my mentor Dr. Wenger. He once described the act of choosing our priorities as being like a pitcher of water and a set of glasses. Imagine you have one pitcher of water on your table and many empty glasses—far more glasses than you could fill with that one pitcher. It's up to you to decide how much water to put in each glass. You could completely fill up one or two glasses and leave the rest empty. Or, you could put just a few inches of water in each one. The only thing you can't do is fill every glass to the top.

What the glasses represent in this analogy is up to you as well. For an athlete, they might represent the Core 4 factors: physical, mental, technical, and tactical. They

It's not enough to stop at "I love my job" or "I want to win." **What is it about winning that you enjoy?**

may have more glasses on their table, too: work, family, hobbies, spiritual health, or any of the other components of a full life.

Whatever the glasses on your table mean to you, one thing is always the same: you only have so much water. We all have a limited capacity. Yes, you can increase it—and I'll talk about that later in this book—but it will never be infinite, and some glasses will have to remain unfilled, at least some of the time. Acknowledging and accepting that your capacity is limited allows you to be realistic in your objectives. When you prioritize which glasses you want to fill, you can more easily allocate how much energy and time you want to give to each one. You may find out you have more time than you think you have for the things that matter.

To create that plan, identify and describe all of the factors that could influence your performance. Then define your performance objectives clearly, openly and honestly, and decide which glasses you need and want to fill. Define what to prioritize, and where to give and take.

Breaking Down Your Objective

Your objective does not stand on its own. There is your objective, and then there are the smaller stages that you need to reach to get there. To reach the first, you have to plan out the second. What exactly do you need to do to get to that space? Athletes in Olympic cycles work with quadrennial (four-year) plans. The support team will ask where the athlete wants to be, and will then create a multi-stage strategic performance plan to get them there.

You likely don't have an Olympic-level support team. So, as a high-performing individual, you have to build your own strategic performance plan. It starts by identifying your personally relevant smaller goals that lie on the way to your objective. What are the steps that will get you there? Who is the team around you who could help?

There are many resources on goal-setting approaches—for example, a popular one is the SMART framework—and there are many tools you can use, from worksheets and flow charts to mind-map templates. But one thing all of these strategies have in common is the need to be honest and clear on what you're committed to and what you prioritize. You may say you want to do something, but in practice you discover that you are not truly committed to it. For example, a person might be interested in fitness, but they aren't working toward any specific fitness goals. There's a difference between being committed and just being interested. If you're fully committed, you're engaged. If that engagement is limited to prioritizing workouts only twice a week, it's important that you understand and appreciate what that commitment level will mean—and what it won't.

THE SMART GOAL FRAMEWORK

SPECIFIC: Your goals are clearly described.

MEASURABLE: Your goals can be tracked and measured.

ACHIEVABLE: Your goals are something you can actually attain.

RELEVANT: Your goals are personally meaningful.

TIME-SENSITIVE: Your goals can be achieved in a realistic and pre-determined timeframe.

Be clear on your priorities and then commit to them within the scope of what you're trying to achieve. If you want to be a high performer, then look at the gaps that exist and the factors that you will to need to enhance. Metrics and key performance indicators (KPI) are very important in determining where you are at with those factors now, and how you are going to get to where you need to be. (I will discuss metrics more in Chapters 6 and 8.) If you're not gifted with a natural ability in any of the Core 4—in whatever form they take for success in your field—then you'd better work on it and make up for any lingering gaps by developing the other three. Are there factors you can work on and improve that could mitigate the detriments to your performance caused by areas you lack? Setting goals and objectives will put you on the path to more focused work and effort.

Lesson Learned

When you are defining your objective, it is not enough to think about what you want to do. What's more important is to think about why you want to do it. If you don't connect your objectives to your *why*, you are going to have a very hard time digging in when things get hard. Don't stop at your first answers—ask yourself deeper and deeper questions until you learn something new about yourself. Knowing why you are working toward an objective will help you weigh all of your competing priorities, and then set a plan to reach that objective.

6

Auditing Your Objective

"Unexpected" success is not the goal. The goal is to match your profile's expected output to the output required to achieve the objective.

TO DEFINE THE OUTPUT required to achieve your objective—that ultimate goal that relates to your why—you first have to audit that objective. Even more than that, you have to audit the objective with respect to *yourself*.

Let me illustrate this with an example. Imagine a cyclist whose objective is to win a specific stage of the Tour de France. Everyone knows that you would need to be a very good bike racer to achieve this, and that, even then—after years of training and thousands of hours spent on a bike developing the ability to put out the necessary wattage—that cyclist might not achieve their objective. There are many gifted and committed cyclists who will never win a single race or stage in their careers. Why? Because there are only so many races and stages, there are thousands of cyclists competing to win them—all of them just as gifted and just as committed as our imaginary cyclist is.

Further, certain courses favor certain types of riders (sprinters, climbers, breakaway specialists, time trialists), and the race day on those courses may take place deep into a Grand Tour (say, day 16 of 21), reducing the number of opportunities to achieve the goal. Performance on a given day and a given course involves far more than strength or stamina or even being able to ride a bike well. All of the Core 4 are always at play: physical, mental, technical, and tactical. On race day, a cyclist isn't just drawing on the physical factor; in fact, some would say that technical, tactical, and (perhaps most of all) mental factors play more of a role in delivering the required output than the physical factors do when the race is on. There have been many times in many races when a rider timed an attack poorly or failed to mentally push through the pain brought on by exhausting themselves during a final climb.

So, the required output for a cyclist isn't just to sustain a target power output over a certain amount of time or to be mentally tough and willing to tolerate pain. It is being able to do all of that in a specific race environment, under competition pressure, when fatigue is setting in, when you're already on the edge and your opponent attacks and you have to make a decisive decision, and...

You get the idea. You've likely been there yourself. Maybe you've had to organize and deliver a presentation for a high-level client when there is a large contract on the line and you've been working overtime for weeks and the competition is gaining traction and the client is questioning the approach—and you didn't have time to eat lunch and there's a missed call on your phone from your kids' school, and...

Just like our racer, you likely had to draw on every one of the Core 4 to make it through and to set yourself up for your best shot at success.

And performance can be demanded of you over the very long term. For our cyclist, it may also be about producing that output at the beginning of the season or after several months of racing, with thousands of kilometers in the legs and a high degree of cumulative fatigue. If they want to deliver the physical, mental, technical, and tactical qualities required in every moment, they will need to make sure they have the capacity to do so. Looking back at Finn Iles and his World Cup race, he had identified the need to be able to sustain his performance level not just in a single race but over the course of the entire race season. That required a capacity to repeatedly deliver high performances again and again, even late into the season, so that he could finish on the podium in the World Cup overall. So, since he *needed* that capacity, he focused on *building* that capacity.

This isn't rocket science, yet it is often misunderstood. I've witnessed many athletes, coaches, and support staff miss this mark—they focused on the demands of a singular event and did not pay enough attention to developing the capacity to perform repeatedly day in, day out, to recover, and to minimize fatigue. However, consistently high-performing athletes and teams do make the connection between sustained performance and capacity. Whatever they do, they do it well, over and over. They understand the output that is required.

Elite sport is a great window through which to view the relationship between the output required and its impact on sustained high performance. At the highest level, the performance objective is often to win, and the variability in performance between competitors becomes so slight as to be nearly negligible. That's why athletes, coaches, and teams are constantly seeking out small windows of opportunity where they can improve the output. In a field where milliseconds matter, each tiny sliver of improvement drives the desire to further analyze the output required to win. Once a part of the coach's job, this type of analysis has evolved into several specialist fields of its own, with professional and Olympic teams often hiring sometimes several different performance analysts to support their coaches and athletes. In every sport that I've been exposed to, I have noticed that the deepest analysis occurs at the highest level of competition and is constantly being optimized by the consistent highest performers. Coaches and athletes, either intuitively or through the intentional investment of time and resources, define the output required to achieve their goals.

I've often been surprised by the level of details these analysts pick up. An excellent example of this is the work

The deepest analysis occurs at the highest level of competition and is constantly being optimized by the consistent highest performers.

led by Sir David Brailsford, the former performance director of British Cycling. His marginal gains approach focuses on the little things that enable the output, not only as discrete actions that can impact performance by small amounts, but also as incremental steps over long periods of time that add up to higher outputs. Each of these little steps contributes to getting an athlete closer to the goal, and when you add them all together, they can produce a big leap. Brailsford's approach requires a very detailed understanding of what the outputs are. His team's execution of that approach and their focus on determining the gaps that can be targeted—along with a significant investment in resources and time—helped Britain become one of the dominant cycling nations in the world.

Fortunately, not all performances require the same level of detail as winning the Tour de France. Most can be improved simply by taking each of the Core 4 and defining the elements that you will need to deliver. Yes, there will always be one-offs and surprise performances where an individual or team reaches their goals without this work, but these are most often caused by luck or serendipity—everything that was needed for that success came together by chance. These one-time winners will not be able to produce consistent and sustainable high performance on demand. Creating a clear picture of what is required for you to achieve the objective sets your benchmark and allows you to assess your current profile against it. It starts a back-and-forth process of comparing your profile to the output required, each time getting you closer to identifying the key attributes you need to deliver.

EVALUATION AND METRICS

Libraries of books have been written about measurement and evaluation and establishing key performance metrics, but there are a few key aspects that are important to understand if you want to ensure you are assessing what you need to assess, in the way you need to assess it. As you read through this chapter and the rest of the book, consider which metrics you might use to evaluate your performance and your profile.

VALIDITY: Does your metric accurately measure what you need it to evaluate? If you put a 100-kilogram weight on a scale, does it measure 100 kilograms? What are the specific key performance indicators (KPIs) that you actually need and that are valid?

RELIABILITY: How consistent is the result when you measure the same thing multiple times? If your true weight is 75 kilograms and you stand on the scale five times, will it register the same weight each time? It is important to understand that a reliable measurement isn't always valid. It may register the same weight every day, but if it says 78 kilograms, that weight would be wrong.

SENSITIVITY: Is your measure sensitive enough to detect changes that are meaningful while not creating excessive "noise"? In other words, is it recording too many changes that aren't relevant to you?

WORTHWHILE CHANGE: Do you know the type of change in the metric that is *worthwhile* to you as it relates to your objective? What is the amount of change that is meaningful to have an impact on your profile or your ability to produce output? This is particularly important when it comes to prioritizing and evaluating the impact of interventions—knowing how much effort needs to go in to get a worthwhile change in output.

Know Your Core 4 Profile

When you are looking at your objective, what will be required physically, mentally, technically, and tactically to produce the necessary output? And what capacity do you currently have in each of those domains? These questions seem simple and logical: *To do X we require Y. So, do we have Y?* Yet accurately understanding your Core 4 profile and the things that limit your output is surprisingly difficult, and it takes time and effort. But it's a commitment worth making, because it will provide personalized context and help you both set realistic expectations and identify areas to improve your profile.

One of the biggest challenges to understanding your Core 4 profile is being honest in your evaluation of what is required and how close you are to it (or, alternatively, how far away you are from it). That's why it's important to surround yourself with individuals who are able and willing to be open and transparent with you. These are the people who will constructively tell you where your gaps in your Core 4 profile exist, and why.

What exactly do I mean when I talk about your Core 4 profile? In sport, we use the word profile to describe the capabilities of an athlete or team. Your profile is your capacity to do something. When it comes to the Core 4—those physical, mental, technical, and tactical factors—your profile is the sum total of how those gears interact with each other. You have a specific capacity for each of the Core 4, and you can increase that capacity through training. That is what we use interventions for.

For example, in the sport world, training an athlete's physical capabilities would include interventions that address injury prevention, rehabilitation, speed, power, strength, conditioning, acceleration, and body composition. We would also work on mental components, like self-efficacy, focus, and the skill sets needed to handle stress and make decisions under pressure. Over time, such work will increase your capacities and change your profile. Some performances will require a degree of emphasis on one of the Core 4 gears, and some will require orchestrated training on all four. A dart-throwing competition taking place in front of an audience of five thousand screaming drunk people, for instance, is a challenge that is very mental and technical, but not very physical. Your emphasis will depend on your objective.

Your profile can change with time, but it won't change overnight. And the change won't always come by intentional design: an older athlete, for example, will have a very different profile from that of their younger self. As a career athlete ages and gains more experience, their technical, tactical, and mental capacities tend to improve; meanwhile, they inevitably start to see a decrease in certain aspects of their physical capacities. For each of us,

Accurately understanding your Core 4 profile and the things that limit your output is surprisingly difficult, **and it takes time and effort.**

our profiles and capabilities will evolve throughout our career: physical maturation, focused training, refining skill, and years of experience all influence and modify our profiles. In some situations, a profile may seem to change quickly, while in others it will take years to develop.

In a team environment, each individual will have their own profile, and the team as a whole will have one as well. Does the team have speed in one area? Is there enough speed across the team to play the way you want to play? Are you a fast team compared to other teams? In any given team or company, you will have multiple "players" in multiple positions, all adding up to a larger picture. Great coaches are good at understanding the profile of their team and using that profile to optimize the output—for example, they might change their tactics depending on the players that they have available. Similarly, great team managers and directors are good at identifying the different player profiles and making changes to alter the profile of their team to produce the output required. They ask themselves questions like: Is there offensive skill in the right positions to play the way we want to play? Are we a high-scoring team compared to the other teams? Do we have the right leadership group and experience to make the right decisions at the right time during competition? The profile for your team might be physically big and strong or very skilled and very small. These two different profiles will lend themselves to different sets of tactics, which will be influenced by your profile as well as the profile of the next team you are set to play—or, in other contexts, by the profile of your competition. (If you think back to Chapter 3, you can see how this highlights the deep importance of understanding integration.)

Every performer will have a certain capacity to produce output on a given day. Take an executive, and think of their Core 4 profile on a Tuesday in May, just as they are approaching the company's year end. Or on a Friday the day after a product launch has wrapped. Or over the course of the entire year. In each of these situations, that executive's technical, tactical, and mental skill sets; their ability to manage stress; how they eat; their physical capacity to recover; their sleep habits; and their travel schedule will all impact their ability to produce an output. Their profile will only be able to deliver so much for a certain period of time—it has a certain capacity. And just like with team sport, their ability to produce output will also be impacted by the profile of the other people in their executive team: the CEO and COO and all the VPs each have their individual profile and objectives that can complement (or conflict with) each other.

Most organizations look at the ability to deliver performance strictly from a technical and tactical perspective. In recent times, the corporate world may have developed a greater appreciation for some of the mental factors, and it's true that some employers do invest in the physical aspects of their employees. But most people and organizations look at those two factors as separate from their performance. Or, they know that mental and physical factors are impacting their performance, but they have no idea how. So let's look at how increasing your capacity within your Core 4 profile actually relates to increasing your output—and, therefore, your performance.

Connecting Output to Your Core 4 Profile

When it is time to perform, your output will be a product of the capacities of your physical, mental, technical, and tactical profiles. Your overall Core 4 profile is what determines both the expected level and the range of your output.

By *level*, I am talking about how well you have developed that capacity in terms of the specific attributes you need: dribbling, speed, leadership, focus, the ability to read the play—whatever the skills are that are relevant to your context. The better developed the attribute, the greater the positive impact on output. When I talk about *range*, I am referring to the day-to-day variability in your performance. For example, an athlete may have great technical skill but below-average aerobic conditioning. In a short match, say a quick three-set tennis match of less than one hour, the athlete can stay fresh and recovered, and so their technical skill can dominate. But in a longer, hard-fought five-set match that lasts nearly three hours, fatigue will set in, and the athlete may not be able to use their technical skill as readily or effectively. The integration is not optimized, and the result is a poorer integrated output. Going match to match, you will see a greater variability in output. Across a narrower range, your output will be more predictable.

You're very rarely going to perform above your profile. And therein lies the connection between profile and expected output. You can't perform above and beyond what's expected if you truly understand your profile. When an athlete hears someone say, "You played better

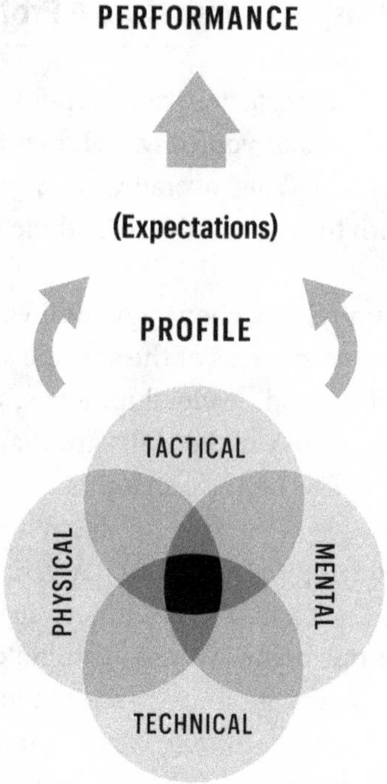

Performance Expectations Relate to Your Profile

than I've ever seen you play before," what that observer is really seeing is the result of a change in the athlete's profile somewhere along the line. (Alternatively, it could be the result of a *moderator* that has influenced the performance, but we will discuss that concept in the next chapter.) What it means is that something has changed—and if it's long term and not a matter of chance, it's your profile. "Unexpected" success is not the goal. The goal is to match your profile's expected output to the output required to achieve the objective.

Aligning Your Output Expectations

I want to dive a little further now into this relationship between performance and expectations. Expectations relate to the output you believe is possible for a given individual or team. In sport, this will be based on the current capacities, the event, and the other athletes who are competing. You determine how good the performance was by evaluating the output against those expectations. Although an expectation may coincide with a dominant, gold-medal performance, it is not related to the outcome (in this case, winning gold) but rather to the output it took to achieve that win. You need to have reason to expect that you are capable of producing the output it takes to win the gold.

When an athlete finishes fifth at the Olympics, this might be viewed as a huge success or as a huge disappointment, depending on the expectations. When it comes to the pundits and the fans in the crowd, the expectations might be completely inappropriate. But for the people supporting that athlete—the people who are *informed*—the expectations should be very clear, and should be based on the output they know the athlete is capable of and prepared to deliver.

To determine whether a performance was up to expectations, you need to be able to clearly evaluate your output.

In a sport like 10K running, this is relatively easy to determine. Physical factors can be measured by speed, stride rate, and physiological outputs (such as heart rate and power); technical factors can be measured by coach observation or video analysis; tactical factors can be measured by pacing execution; and mental factors can be measured by decision-making or self-evaluation. All of these together provide an overall evaluation of performance output. Which, as you know by now, has nothing to do with how that athlete placed in the event—in other words, it has nothing to do with the outcome.

It's unrealistic to expect someone to perform at a personal-best level in every performance. All performances have a ceiling—no one can continue to get better and better results each time they perform. However, it is reasonable to have a range of outputs that would still be classified as high performance. The more often you perform (daily versus weekly versus monthly), the wider the range will be in your expected performance output, and the lower the level relative to the maximal ceiling. The key is to make sure that the entire range is at a high enough level to deliver an output as often as necessary that is capable of meeting your performance objectives.

Take for example a professional soccer team that plays a very aggressive and physically demanding game. One of the key metrics for them to defend properly is to be able to cover a lot of ground every game—more than the rest of the teams in their league—so that their shape makes it very difficult for the opposition to break them down. They have to hit a minimum level of output each

Invest the time to be strategic—to determine what you're doing, why you're doing it, and what order it comes in priority.

game to maintain their defensive shape, with limited rest and recovery from training and competition. But, if they are well prepared, this is not necessarily their maximal output. If it were, they would not be able to deliver that output consistently in a congested schedule due to fatigue and a lack of recovery.

It is not unlike a sales executive's ability to deliver a high-quality sales pitch on a regular basis. If, as that executive, you are presenting one of these pitches each month and have enough time to prepare a good presentation on your own, the quality of the presentation will be high. If you have to deliver a pitch each week, your ability to prepare each one may be slightly reduced; then, even more so if you have to present a new pitch every few days. The more frequently you have to produce them, the less preparation time you will have, and the lower the quality of the presentation will be. Sure, they may still be good, but they will not be *as* good. Expected output is determined by your Core 4 profile. High performers can produce an output at their expected level on demand. Performance should only be measured against the output required to achieve the objective when the expected output of your specific profile matches or exceeds it. If it doesn't, it is time to identify your gaps and prepare a plan to modify your profile and ensure it has the required capacity.

Identifying Your Core 4 Gaps

One of my goals in this book is to help people in all fields understand the process of producing sustainable performances—an area of focus that is very well understood in sport but often lacking in so many other areas of our society. Admittedly, the sheer number of ways in which you can break down performance can be overwhelming. How deep do you need to go to determine the output required and identify the gaps in your capabilities?

In my experience, everyone has at least a general understanding of what is required for their own personal performance. Where people often get handcuffed is when it's time to dig down into a more comprehensive level of detail to describe the output required and prioritize their key areas of focus. More often than not, people think they need to do everything.

To break out of that mind block, start by deconstructing the specific problems that are occurring within the Core 4 performance factors. Some gears may have more influence than others at different times, and some of your priorities may seem to contradict each other. It might seem like you need to develop multiple aspects of performance all at once, which can leave you feeling like you can't tackle them all. So, invest the time to be strategic—to determine what you're doing, why you're doing it, and what order it comes in priority. Think of that table full of glasses and the one pitcher of water you have to fill them with. Which glasses do you want to fill, and how much do you want to put in each one? What are the most crucial gaps that are limiting your output? Don't separate yourself from what you do: when you are analyzing the gaps and prioritizing your efforts, you need to look at yourself and your work (or your sport, or your creative pursuit...) as a single individual—a combination of both.

This will all take work. But if you want to truly understand what is impacting your performance, you have to do it. Start with the top two or three elements in each of the Core 4 that you feel are most important—the ones you cannot deliver the output without. They must also be personal, and relative to your objective. If you are a midfielder in soccer, the technical skills you need to be a high performer include passing or tackling skills (and those skills will be different depending on whether you are a defensive versus an attacking midfielder). And if you are a CFO, the technical skills you need will include reading, interpreting, and analyzing complex financial statements. You will need other specific skills for the tactical and mental factors—and (in more cases than you'd think) for the physical factors as well.

Next, ask yourself whether you have the capacity to deliver these outputs already. If you don't, then that is your starting point—you have identified a gap. Don't get caught up in the finer details until you have closed this gap.

The Sustainability Element

Once you have closed a gap, it's time to ask yourself if you are delivering that aspect of your output on demand consistently in the specific environment. If your answer is yes, then you can move on to look for gaps in a different area. If your answer is no, you need to ask why and determine what piece of being able to produce the output is missing.

An example of this is a hockey player who has a very high level of offensive technical skill to pass and shoot to create scoring opportunities. They have more than enough capacity to deliver the output on a technical level and to show it at times in games, but they can't do it consistently. If they were to focus solely on their technical work, such as improving their already adequate shooting or passing, they are not addressing the real gap—they are just building excess capacity. What they need to do is to ask themselves why they are underperforming in competition. Perhaps they are starting off well in their games but fading out later when they are tired. Or perhaps they don't get tired but they are hitting a gap in certain levels of competition where the speed of play and decision-making is just a fraction of a second quicker. By breaking down the output a little further, they might realize that the gap is not technical but rather physical or mental. Or, it might be an issue with integration: they need to improve how they apply their technical skill in environments that require quicker decision-making.

As you get more detailed in identifying and analyzing a critical gap, you will likely begin to see how the Core 4 factors influence each other: how physical factors can limit your mental abilities, or how your tactical plans can lead you to fall short on delivering your technical skills. Keep on repeating the process of identifying gaps in output and analyzing which factors are most likely the true cause until you have identified six to eight key outputs that you need your Core 4 profile to have the capacity to produce.

Lesson Learned

Once you have identified your objective, it's time to define the actual outputs required and audit how well you are currently positioned to meet them. Be honest, and get specific. Take a hard look at your Core 4 performance factors and any problems or gaps that are occurring within them. Use metrics to measure those gaps and the progress you are making in closing them. Make sure any progress you make is sustainable. And understand how all the factors are influencing each other to support or undermine your performance.

7

Moderators and Interventions

Your profile is not static—
you can always develop it further.

AS WITH most things in life, the relationship between your Core 4 profile and your output is constantly in flux. The profile of every individual and every team is not static but dynamic, always changing because of injury, physical or technical training, travel, the competitive landscape, new team members—there are countless details that can influence the expected output on any given day. People often get overwhelmed thinking about all the permutations that could impact either their profile or their expected output. It can feel like you're constantly trying to hit a moving target.

To simplify this process, I like to bucket all of these various influencers into two categories: *moderators* and *interventions*. Moderators are those factors that have a short-term impact on the output: they typically come and go. Interventions are the opposite: they are facilitating your performance on any given day, changing or raising your profile for a sustained, ongoing change. Interventions can be aimed at increasing your capacity in any one of the Core 4. It is critical to consider both moderators and interventions when you are creating your plan to match your profile to the output required. Let's take a deeper look at each.

Moderators

When working with both athletes and executives, I often see people get frustrated as they try to account for those performance-affecting factors that seem random or are only occasionally important. These factors can affect—or moderate—a performance in positive and negative ways, and they can come in a variety of forms: they can be operational (scheduling, travel, altitude, weather, jet lag, canceled flights, project deadlines) or situational (illness, injury, stress, lack of sleep); they can be directly related to the output (a personality clash on your team) or not (an illness in your family). People will often frame these moderators as "one-offs" or special situations, or even use them to explain away a poor result. "That was unpredictable!" they might tell me. "How could I account for that?"

Certainly, wild cards and disruptions like these can make it challenging to predict the exact performance output, no matter how well you know the Core 4 profile of the people or teams involved. If a family member gets in an accident or a child is sick the night before a big event, that will affect the performance. But the effect of moderators like these is transient: when the moderating element is gone or avoided—if you reschedule the event or catch up on your sleep, for example—the expected output should go back to normal. And, to some degree, you can also anticipate them—you can build back-up plans or improve your capacity to build leeway into your profile by developing the mental and tactical skills that will allow you to pivot for an unexpected event.

The number and variety of moderators you might come across in a given field of performance is infinite, but in my experience in sport I find that they can often be categorized into four categories: environment, fatigue, recovery, and travel. All of these categories can have surprising applications in the non-sport world, so they are worth further discussion.

Environment

Environmental moderators can be physical or social. Physical examples include weather (rain, snow, fog), temperature, altitude, and the facility the performance is taking place in. Imagine the impact of rain on a downhill mountain biker's output on a given course, or how traveling to an away game where the temperature is 20 degrees warmer will affect the performance of a football team—fatigue from heat exposure can be significant if the players are not acclimated. Likewise, imagine a lacrosse

Certain responses
are relative to
certain environments.
**So, know your
environment.**

team that always prepares and plays on grass but must play an important match on turf where the ball moves and bounces differently. If they are unable to practice on turf prior, their expected output may be impacted.

I once worked with a high-caliber athlete who had already achieved significant success but was having trouble performing at altitude—for some athletes, a higher altitude than they are accustomed to can impact hydration, hunger, recovery, and more. For this athlete, it was affecting her sleep, especially in the first four days. We adjusted her training loads for those first days, and got her a private room so she could sleep easier and more soundly.

Without examination, some might have concluded that this athlete had sleeping challenges or just couldn't perform at altitude. But she didn't have a sleep challenge, she had a challenge sleeping at altitude while she was acclimating. Certain responses are relative to certain environments. So, know your environment. Many aspects within it will be dynamic and changeable. The good news is that, other than sudden changes in weather, moderators from this category are usually predictable and can be managed quite well with good preparation and planning. In the case of the athlete, with that planning and preparation she was able to adjust and improve her outputs at altitude.

Your social environment can also have a direct influence on your ability to deliver an output. I've witnessed many athletes deliver a less-than-expected performance as a result of a change in the team around them. Imagine a dispute between two players, or a team leader disagreeing with the approach of a coach for a specific game. Both situations can lead to a lack of trust or commitment in effort, or distract other team members.

The social aspect is also at play in your work environment. I've watched athletes, or people from their inner circles, get so caught up in the excitement of an Olympic event that they lose their focus on their performance. The Olympics is an intense event with thousands of the world's best athletes, coaches, and practitioners all living in close proximity, with family, friends, media, and fans all wanting to share the experience. That's why national Olympic committees plan familiarization visits; do extensive media training; implement policies on social media access, visitation, and family visits; and even provide optional accommodations outside of the village—it is all designed to proactively minimize any environmental factors that could impact the athletes' abilities to perform. The social environment in a given workplace may not always be as intense as at an Olympic Games, but we all have connections with family, partners, friends, and co-workers, and those connections can affect our performance in a thousand ways. Breaking up with a partner, a family member falling ill, having a disagreement with a colleague—these can all lead to distraction, anxiety, stress, and loss of focus. The social environment of a workplace can also influence performance both negatively and positively—look back on your own experience and consider the effects of factors like office buddies, inside jokes, positive teamwork, networking, brainstorming, office gossip, and so on.

Having the right culture and aligning that culture with action is critical to sustained high performance. Any short-lived change in culture can destroy even the best strategies and have direct effects on output. While culture takes time to build through action and I wouldn't typically classify it as transient, I have seen cultural factors act as moderators, both negatively and positively. You've likely witnessed yourself that a change in leadership or the arrival of a new team member can have a big impact on a team. While the culture of the organization may be strong, the introduction of a new member who has a different attitude or isn't aligned with the rest of the team can lead to a short-term breakdown in output. Conversely, the removal of a team member who was unknowingly acting as a block to the output of other team members can result in an improved performance. I recall discussing this aspect of moderators with an executive from a national organization that had just experienced the removal of a senior leader. The change led to a dramatic increase in the productivity of this executive's department—staff were more engaged and were exhibiting a much higher sense of alignment with the company. This is not uncommon, and it can become even more evident in cases where the leader who departed suddenly returns and the output drops back to its previous level. It is one of the reasons why consistently high-performing cultures are very careful about who they bring into their team and are quick to make changes when they discover something that negatively impacts their ability to deliver. Think about situations in your own performance where the social environment has either positively or negatively impacted output.

Fatigue

It's fairly intuitive that a higher fatigue state will usually result in a lower physical output in most sports. Conversely, increased recovery time—within reason!—will typically enhance your ability to deliver physically. The impact of fatigue on your ability to perform will depend on your capacity and the output required. If your performance output is heavily dependent on a physical capacity, and that capacity is matched identically to that required output, any excess fatigue is going to have a big impact.

Let me illustrate this by comparing a 10K runner to a basketball player. Running a 10K in a highly competitive time (under twenty-eight minutes for men or thirty minutes for women) requires a very refined physiological engine that is near the athlete's maximal abilities. An athlete will want to match their ability to run their absolute fastest with their most important race of the season. If they are carrying any fatigue, they will not be able to deliver their best performance on the day that they need to deliver it. Our basketball player, meanwhile, requires only a certain physical profile to play twenty-five to thirty-five minutes per game, some of which depends on their individual style of play. Their performance is less dependent on having maximal physical capabilities in any one area, which is part of why they can play so well in eighty-two games over a regular season. It also creates an opportunity for excess capacity; players with additional capacity typically take longer to fatigue and can play more when teams must play multiple games in a short period of time.

If you're thinking that fatigue doesn't apply to you and your work, you are wrong. Fatigue doesn't just affect our physical outputs, it affects the technical, tactical, and mental attributes of our performance, too. Tired people have compromised abilities to perform technical operations, make decisions, and handle stress or pressure. We can all relate to being overtired and making mistakes or being irritable. An athlete who is fatigued late in a game or in the final game of a best-of-seven playoff series is more likely to make poor decisions, and a project manager in crunch time after a long contract who is fatigued is going to make poor decisions, too. Forward-thinking programs and organizations realize the importance of fatigue management for all key decision-makers. All of your painstaking preparation can be thrown away when an overtired or stressed team member makes a poor decision in a key moment.

Recovery

Recovery strategies have been a hot topic for the last twenty years. They have spawned an entire industry, both within sport and in daily life. In elite sport you see it in recovery clothing (compression garments) and high-tech equipment (pneumatic compressors, cold tubs, cryochambers), but anywhere else you look you'll see sleep tracking apps, activity monitors and watches, nutritional supplements and creams—all flooding in to capitalize on this ever-growing market. Companies are spending millions on developing artificial intelligence engines to interpret personal data and biometrics and provide recovery recommendations, all to help us "recover" from stressors so we can optimize our output.

While each of these innovations may have a place in the right context, they are what I refer to as supplemental strategies. They are only helpful after you've adequately addressed the recovery triad: *sleep*, *rest*, and *nutrition*. These fundamental aspects of recovery are interconnected and have significant moderating effects on output.

If you take any one factor from this triad out of your recovery equation, you will be less likely to get optimal recovery. You could be eating and sleeping well, but if you're not resting from an intense period of energy expense (physical or mental), you may end up being overstressed and fatigued. You could be sleeping and resting well, but if you're eating poorly, you're not going to adapt and recover properly, nor will you have the energy to perform when required. Each part of this triad functions together, and each part is important. Here's why:

Sleep: Sleep plays a significant role in recovery. This is when your body physiologically restores many of its systems back to homeostasis—it is where a lot of physical adaptation occurs. Studies have connected adequate sleep to improvements in reaction time, decision-making, and physical outputs. (The exact ideal amount of time naturally depends on the individual and the performance objective—the range is usually from seven to nine hours

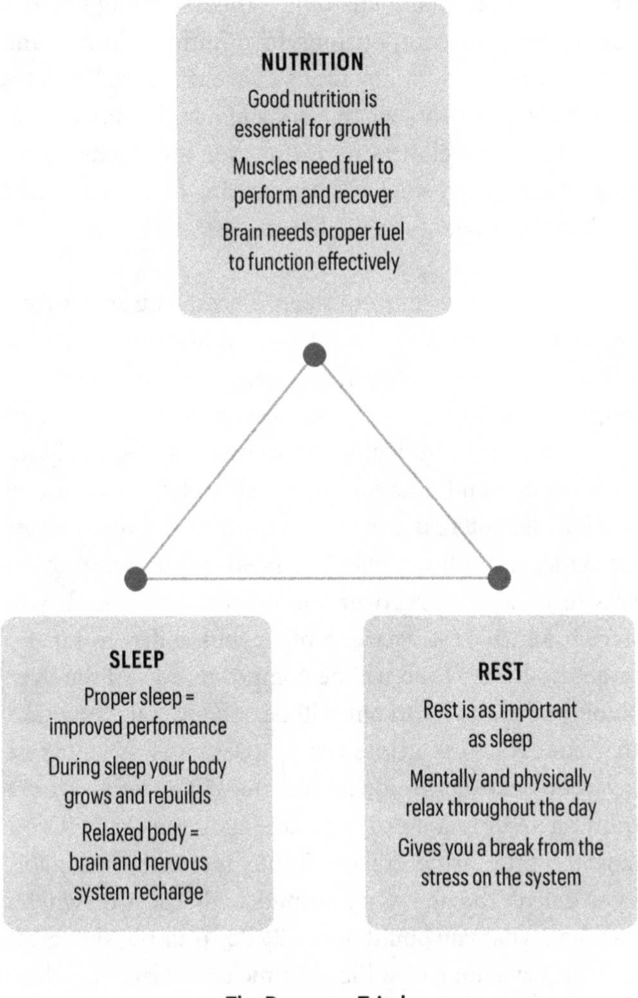
NUTRITION
Good nutrition is essential for growth
Muscles need fuel to perform and recover
Brain needs proper fuel to function effectively
SLEEP
Proper sleep = improved performance
During sleep your body grows and rebuilds
Relaxed body = brain and nervous system recharge
REST
Rest is as important as sleep
Mentally and physically relax throughout the day
Gives you a break from the stress on the system

The Recovery Triad

a night for adults.) It is common practice in sport to track an athlete's sleep and customize their sleeping environments prior to competitions to minimize fatigue and optimize recovery. Many times I have witnessed athletes and executives who average six and a half hours a night marvel at how well they perform when they focus on getting better quality sleep or by increasing that sleep period by as little as twenty to thirty minutes.

Rest: This is different from sleep. To rest, you are awake—but you are also taking a break from your work or training regimen to relax, refresh, and recover. When you rest, your body and mind recharge. Rest influences your ability to recovery physically and mentally to be ready for the next demand. Imagine you're an athlete in a training session and you're doing five times three minutes of exercise at a certain heart rate. You need rest between those sets to be able to recover and do the next one. If you have too little rest between reps, your ability to hit the target in the next rep will be compromised and the overall output of that workout will be suboptimal. Now take that concept to multiple training sessions. If your rest between sessions is adequate, you will enter that next training session able to complete it as required. If you have too little rest and haven't fully recovered, your ability to deliver the necessary outputs in that session will be less than what you could normally do. Your physiological systems have not had sufficient time to return to baseline or adapt. This same concept applies to your mental load, and to your ability to manage stress over the long term.

Nutrition: This is the last piece of the recovery triad. You may be working hard in your physical activities or training program, or perhaps you're focused on being able to perform at an elite business level. But how often do you focus on nutrition and its ability to impact your performance? As a moderator, nutrition can have a direct impact on your ability to deliver the output in the days leading up to a performance—affecting your energy stores, recovery, and alertness as you prepare—and during the performance itself. Poor nutrition can cause large swings in your blood glucose levels and hormonal responses, leading to potentially negative impacts on your cognitive function and energy availability. Your brain can't make effective decisions, and your muscles will struggle to do the work. Those headaches may be caused by poor hydration levels or because you are running low on fuel. Your brain and body cannot function effectively without good nutrition. You can perform optimally in sport, at home, and at work if you fuel your body with healthy food and avoid excess sugar, fat, alcohol, and unhealthy foods. A healthy and well-planned diet also provides nutrients for growth and development.

I find this to be a significant challenge for so many people. We all eat every day so, in a sense, we are all experts in eating. But understanding *eating* is not the same as understanding *nutrition*, or its impacts on performance. Physiology is complex, and how the body absorbs, uses, and responds to different nutritional approaches will be different for everyone. When I'm working with clients, I always recommend speaking with a registered dietitian who has experience in understanding the nutritional needs of supporting performance and health.

If you pay attention to these three recovery pieces, your body will adapt and bounce back from the stressors and loads you are placing on it.

Travel

Travel can be tough on both the mind and the body. Although it is related to both fatigue and recovery, it deserves to be discussed on its own. The impacts of travel are often short-lived but can sometimes persist for several days. One of the most significant travel considerations is jet lag. I think the best description I've heard for jet lag in sport came from Dr. Ralph Mistlberger, a professor of cognitive and neural sciences at Simon Fraser University and the director of the Sleep and Circadian Neuroscience Lab. Like most of us, Dr. Mistlberger links the *lag* part of the term to changing time zones. Your body is used to waking up at a certain time, and so time zone changes affect your chronobiology and circadian rhythms. When you travel across continents or multiple time zones, you can potentially get into a scenario where your circadian rhythm almost inverts on itself. You end up waking up in the middle of the night and feeling tired during the day, resulting in a significant impact on your output. An added pressure is the fact that long-haul intercontinental flights are often designed to arrive early in the morning, leaving you with an entire day before you get on the plane, plus an extended full day on arrival. You may have to get up earlier than normal to catch a

I've watched athletes
get so caught up
in the excitement of an
Olympic event that they
**lose their focus on their
performance.**

morning flight, or miss a day of preparation. That all results in added stress, contributing further to fatigue.

What's more interesting is that Dr. Mistlberger links the *jet* part to the underappreciated effect of the travel itself on your body: time in a confined space (often crammed into a small seat), minimal fresh air, lack of privacy (a stressor for introverted people), minimal good food choices, immigration and security checks, worry about making it to the departure gate on time, and all of the other disruptions involved in long-distance travel. It's not like you've gone out and run a marathon or finished a hard training session, but these combined stressors still have a significant effect. On the physical side, when you're flying in a plane at 35,000 feet, the air pressure inside the cabin is adjusted to simulate altitude of 6,000 to 8,000 feet to ensure safe travel and maintain the pressure on the hull. The altitude that reduced oxygen pressure simulates is still very high and has a physiological impact on your body, which adds to all of those other stressors (particularly that of being in a confined space for an extended period of time with limited movement). Practical travel strategies and tools are available from travel clinics, credible online sources, and even your doctor. Aerobic fitness can also help with managing this moderator (something I'll touch on in the next chapter). If you are required to travel as part of your performance, I recommend considering how you might plan to manage its potential impacts.

The Performance Window

While there are many moderators that can impact output, the extent of their impact depends on what you do in the days before your performance. In sport, we often look at the seventy-two-hour window prior to competition, making sure that we are reducing the likelihood of a moderator influencing the output during that time. Dr. David Cox, a sport psychologist and colleague of mine, refers to this as the "performance window." It represents the period of time leading up to a performance in which what you do influences your state of readiness to perform.

Take for example a team competing in professional sport: with all else being equal, the output expected for a team that has three days off prior to a match would be greater than the output expected in the fourth match in five days. Similarly, if you have not slept well for several days or you had to stay up all night with a sick child the night before an important day at work, your fatigue will likely moderate your expected output. This window is an opportunity for you to ensure that you are minimizing any negative impacts of fatigue, poor recovery (sleep, nutrition, rest), travel, condensed scheduling, distractions, and stressors. Naturally, each person's context will be different, and, depending on your situation, you may not have the full seventy-two hours to use. But it is important to understand that everything you do during this time has the potential to positively or negatively impact your output. If you have to travel for a big presentation, try to go a few days early if you can. Likewise, make sure you have good sleeps leading up to a big work day just in case you have a poor sleep the night before.

One last note about moderators. At some point, moderators such as travel or environment can transition to become part of the required output. If you find you are having to travel regularly (for example, like a professional basketball player, airline pilot, or regional manager would) or that something external is requiring your ongoing attention (say, having a child or caring for an aging parent), the required output for your objective has changed. Or, if your performance objective is a one-off event—an Olympic competition in the heat; orchestrating an international industry conference—you must consider the moderator as part of the required output.

Think about your own performance and the key times in which you need to perform. How do you typically manage fatigue and recovery in the days prior? Do you pay attention to other moderators and their influence on your output? Most of us don't tend to think this way with respect to how we perform daily in our careers or personal lives, but if we want to maximize our performance, we should start taking these factors into account. To perform on demand at a high level consistently, you must be able to identify, manage, and account for the moderators. Fortunately, many moderators can be mitigated by proper planning and preparation. By addressing the individual gears of performance in your Core 4 profile, you can increase your ability to effectively deal with moderators.

Interventions

As humans, we are adaptable, emotional beings with the ability to learn, and we have high levels of cognitive function. The physiologist in me would say that we are a series of systems that interact in a variety of ways that allow us to learn, grow, move, think, adapt, and respond to various stimuli in our environments. These systems work together to produce outputs in everything we do. At times they can be simple, straightforward, and predictable, while at other times they can be complex in their interactions. These systems are modifiable to a certain degree that is determined by genetics and other factors outside your control—yet very few people have developed their capacities in the physical, mental, technical, and tactical domains to their theoretical maximal capacity. My experience has been that most people, including elite performers—athletes, artists, leaders, academics—have additional bandwidth in one or more of the Core 4 areas. Your profile is not static—you can always develop it further.

I like to refer to the training and practices that we use to develop our Core 4 profiles as interventions. We use interventions with purpose to expand our profiles and build our capacities to produce output. Interventions typically have a longer-term component to them in that they produce change that is more resilient and stable, and less transient. They also take longer to develop. Examples of interventions in sport would include the months of technical practice required to execute a freestyle ski trick, or the regular ongoing training in the gym to have the strength and power to prevent a rushing linebacker from tackling your quarterback. Likewise, the professional development an accountant will undertake in order to understand the technical work of tax planning is an intervention that is stable and that increases their capacity.

An intervention may also act more indirectly by impacting the effectiveness of another intervention. A good example of this would be when an athlete works on their nutrition and strength training simultaneously. If the goal of the strength training is to increase maximal strength, while the goal of the nutrition regimen is to manage body composition and weight, the athlete and their support team need an integrated approach to designing these two interventions. By including a quality meal plan that coincides with strength training, you can influence the impact of that program to produce adaptations over a training phase. Likewise, the strength program may influence the effectiveness of the nutrition program to reach body composition or weight goals. These gains may be better or worse for either depending on how the interventions have been designed. This is another case where integration—the blending of one aspect with another—is something you need to consider.

Interventions can also be influenced by moderators. Because many interventions—learning team tactics, developing speed or power—have specific actions associated with them, they can be considered as mini performances. You are required to do something in order to gain the benefit to build your capacity. As with

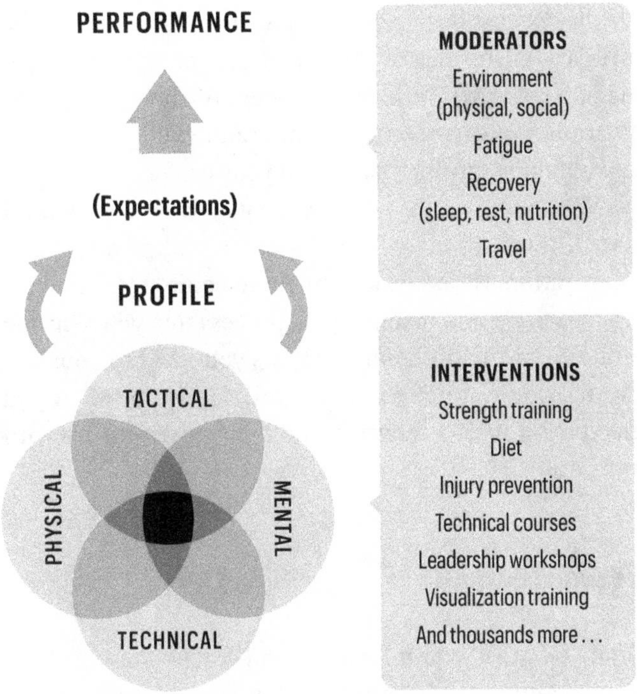

Moderators and Interventions Impact Performance

performance, moderators can influence your ability to execute on the task required by the intervention. Imagine a basketball player trying to focus on shooting practice when dealing with family stress, or having to attend a hard, team-based tactical session following a poor night's sleep after a late night out on the town. These moderators will compromise the effectiveness of those sessions.

While success in a given practice session may not be the primary performance objective, one poor session can negatively impact the effectiveness of the overall intervention. Do this too many times and you'll reduce the likelihood of closing that gap in your profile.

While all of these factors may start to feel complicated, they can be managed with careful planning and preparation. In the final chapters to come, I will present a preparation and roadmapping process that will help you unite all of the different elements you need to consider, so that you can define the output, determine what you need to be able to deliver it, and then move forward with purpose.

Lesson Learned

To deliver the required output and reach your objective, you are going to have to develop your Core 4 profile. Interventions are the specific actions you take to execute that development: the specific training regimens and education plans you undertake to get you where you need to be. It may sound obvious, but more things are influencing your output than you know—including the key moderators of rest, recovery, and nutrition.

PART 3

PERFORMANCE IN ACTION

8

The Role of Preparation

Purposeful preparation leads to performance on demand.

IF YOU want to be able to execute your required output on demand—to put your performance into action—you first need to pursue excellence in preparation. Preparation is the sum of all the various interventions you undertake to address the physical, mental, technical, and tactical gaps in your performance. It is about controlling the things you can control.

For an intervention to have an impact on your performance, you need two things. First, the intervention must be effective at improving the specific capacity you are targeting within your Core 4 profile. Is your training program increasing your aerobic capacity? Your dexterity? Your coding skills? Second, the interventions must translate into the specific improvements you need in your performance. Does that heightened aerobic capacity improve your fatigue tolerance during a hockey game? Does better dexterity improve your craftwork? Does that better coding knowledge result in fewer bugs? Determining the right interventions is where things can get a bit murky, and that murkiness can lead to variability in opinions and approaches. As humans, we like to simplify and draw connections to help us make sense of things that are difficult to understand. Sometimes simplification is effective, but other times it isn't.

This tendency to want to simplify things also leads us to give weight to various anecdotes we hear on what the best interventions are, how best to eat, or what path we should take to get to our objectives. We see someone achieve goals that we think are similar to ours, so we look to simulate or replicate what they did. This is why so many people choose strategies used by famous athletes, influencers, or friends—they believe or hope that what worked for someone else will work for them. It's easier to choose an intervention that we've seen someone else use than it is to think through and prioritize the most appropriate choices for our own objective. I've seen this lead to many mistakes in both sport and personal performance. That doesn't mean you can't learn from others' experiences, but you do need to think critically about if and how they relate to you. Optimizing your output requires you to personalize your own plan and your own interventions. Your interventions need to be specific to your needs and sufficient to change the underlying attribute of the profile you're trying to change. And then they have to translate to your specific performance output.

In elite sport, savvy athletes and their support teams will always incorporate *specificity of training* into their interventions. Specificity of training refers to an approach that simulates what is required in the output. This can range from simulating a single movement of the performance (such as a single leg squat in a skating stride pattern for a hockey player) to simulating the entire performance as closely as possible (such as conditioning a hockey team with competitive scrimmages and shifts that mimic shift duration and recovery periods). In the business world you might see this when a sales rep repeats and repeats their pitch in front of a group of colleagues, or in theater when an actor walks through a particular action again and again on stage during rehearsal. By designing your intervention to simulate your performance as closely as possible, you are trying to best predict the ability of your intervention to have an impact on your output.

This likely makes intuitive sense for you, and in many situations it can be an effective approach. But if that is all you focus on, it can limit your ability to adapt your profile. What if an exact simulation of the activity doesn't provide enough of a stimulus for adaptation to occur? You may already be the fittest player on the ice and the challenge is limited by everyone else. Or, alternatively, you may be the least fit player on the ice, and trying to keep up with everyone creates so much fatigue in the early minutes that you're not able to do the rest of the session with any intensity. That fatigue may even have

Each of your interventions should have an impact on your ability to produce output. **If they don't, they are not a priority.**

unintended consequences on other aspects of your performance, such as quality repetition of technical skills. The person the sales rep is pitching to may find the delivery flat and over-rehearsed. You've put significant effort and work into repeating what you will be doing in the performance, and yet this may have had very little impact on either the attribute you're trying to improve or the final performance itself. So, to reach high performance, you need a purposeful approach. Purposeful preparation leads to performance on demand.

Planning and Prioritization

It's important to note that you won't be able to address all of your gaps at the same time, or right away. We all have a limited amount of time in our days, weeks, and months, and so you will need to plan. Your plan must prioritize not only which gaps you want to address first, but also which interventions you will use to best address those gaps.

Naturally, each individual will have different needs to take into account in their plan, and will have to prioritize different interventions and build in different approaches. But there are still some common aspects that are fundamental to any effective preparation plan. You don't need to be an expert planner to adequately address these aspects and prepare for your objective. You only need to ask yourself some specific questions, and be very honest about the answers:

- How much of a priority is the factor I am changing (high or low)?
- Does the intervention have an impact on other aspects of my performance (for example, physical influences on technical capacity)?
- How big will the impact of this intervention be (small or large)?
- How much will I have to do to make that impact (a lot or a little)?
- What is the net performance impact of this action (positive or negative)?

If you don't have a lot of experience with highly competitive sport, that final point may not be familiar to you. But it is a critical factor in prioritizing your interventions, so let's take a closer look at it.

The Importance of Net Performance Impact

When prioritizing interventions, it's important to think of them in terms of their relative impact on your output. A big part of this is understanding how malleable a given attribute is. Some interventions require a high level of detail and thus demand significant resources, while others are simpler or more flexible. Does the capacity you're trying to modify have a big enough bandwidth for change? How much has to be done to get the needle to move a particular amount? Can a little bit of work lead to a lot of bandwidth change? What is the performance impact for the effort you will have to put into it? Do you get lots for little, or a little for lots? It helps to be clear on the priorities of each factor relative to what needs to be done and to the context of the situation. Each of your interventions should have an impact on your ability to produce output. They should be purposeful and have a performance impact. If they don't, they are not a priority.

Net performance impact is an approach that helps you make this assessment—it measures the net return of all the various interventions in your preparation. It's similar to how you need to account for all of your revenues, expenses, taxes, and interest when you are determining net income; when you are assessing your intervention choices, you need to account both for the potential benefits and for the potential "take-aways" or compromises that might arise from them. These choices need to consider the net performance impact relative to the objective.

You can see an example of this in youth sport, where the coaches have a limited number of contact hours with their teams. A coach might identify gaps in the technical skills, overall conditioning (physical), and tactical understanding across the developing players on the team. From there, they have to determine where to best spend the limited time available based on what needs to be done to close these gaps. Some coaches may look to spend time on all three areas, developing a bit of each but not maximizing any one. Others may focus on tactics, so that the team becomes very good in running a system that is difficult for their opponents to break down, even though technical or physical development for the individual players may fall behind. Yet another coach may look to spend all of their time trying to optimize only the physical and technical factors, and not worry about tactics. Their players may end up being better athletes in two to three years, but may not be as successful as a team in the short term.

A couple of things are important to note here. First, your preparation must purposefully relate back to your performance objective, and that is personal to you—in our youth league example, not all coaches will have the same performance objective. Second, the specific areas you choose to work on and how you design their interventions must be prioritized with respect to the net performance impact for the efforts you put in. Here's what I mean: let's say one of those youth league coaches wants to work on all three areas, and let's assume they have six hours per week to address those gaps. How will they divide the time? Let's assume they commit two hours to each area, equating to a 10 percent, 12 percent, and 15 percent potential improvement in physical, technical, and tactical, respectively. Responses and adaptation times will be different between interventions, and so the hours of effort the team has to put into each of the three areas will not be equal. Using a net performance approach, our hypothetical coach would ask: *If we took thirty minutes away from physical and put it into technical, would the gain in technical as it relates to the performance objective be greater than the loss in physical?* If the answer is yes, then that change will increase the net performance impact more than keeping the two factors equal would.

As another example, let's say you hold a leadership role in your organization and want to train for a running race while maintaining both the quality of your work and your family involvement. This is your performance objective. Both your job and home life are busy, but you are managing and performing well. You hire a running coach who provides you with a detailed and extensive program, outlining the times of day to train, the numbers you need to hit, how many hours of sleep you need to get, and how many sessions you have to do per week. The emphasis is on intensity work, which has been shown to maximize adaptation and training response for hours of effort put in. The program also includes nutrition recommendations to optimize your response to the training.

While this may be a very good program for getting a runner fit for the time put in, what is the net performance impact? The extensive details and programming may add a layer of stress or excessive fatigue that negatively influences your work and home life. Your overall performance relative to your objective may drop. It doesn't matter how good the plan is or how well-tailored the interventions are—if it becomes too much for you, you will not achieve your overall performance objective. You will start to miss workouts, recover less, and not optimize the effectiveness of the program. Furthermore, the interventions for running (one piece of the performance objective) will begin to have a negative impact on your work and home life (the other pieces of the performance objective), resulting in a negative overall effect on the net performance impact.

By modifying your program slightly to be more flexible in scheduling and targeting some lower-intensity work to help with recovery, reduce fatigue, and reduce overall stress, you may end up being more compliant because you can fit it all in and you are feeling better about the approach. You will increase your run fitness while still maintaining performance at work and at home. If the program is designed well, you may actually see improvements in your workplace due to higher energy levels, improved overall fitness, and the self-confidence that comes along with it. You may even find you sleep better.

Creating Your Schedule

Once you are ready to build your plan, the next step is to look at key items as they relate to your schedule. The first thing you need to do is to identify all of the uncontrollable items that are related to your objective or that will require your time. These are the things you will not be able to manipulate unless your objective changes.

In Olympic-level sport, for example, the athletes can't control the date of the Olympic Games. They have only a set amount of time to prepare. Full stop. They also can't control the selection criteria or the events they have to compete in to get selected for the Olympic team. In professional sport, the players can't control the pre-season

You can't manage a constraint **until you identify it.**

date start or the season schedule. Teams can make their own travel choices, but they can't get around the travel required to get to and from away matches. What they *can* control is the effort they put out, and (for the most part) how well prepared they are for each match.

When it comes to planning for your preparation for your objective, there are going to be things that are out of your control, too. All you can do is accept them and deal with them. Many of us must travel or commute for our jobs, work certain hours, or care for family members. You might want to take a course to develop your technical skills, but the classes may only occur on specific dates, or it may be some other form of constraint. Some may be changeable, but many may not. When you come up against an uncontrollable constraint, you will have to evaluate what can be changed around that constraint to better manage it. Can you start work at a different time to avoid traffic? Can you do more meetings on video conference to limit travel? Can you take the course online?

You can't manage a constraint until you identify it, so take the time to brainstorm and define as many of the uncontrollable pieces as you can. Write them out on a timeline or a calendar so you can look at the big picture. This work will give you a rough schedule and will help you identify where you could place your interventions around the things that are out of your control. More than that, it will help you clarify what is realistic and how much time you actually have to prepare for your performance. The first time you do this, it can be quite a reality check—you may realize that you won't be able to change as many things as you thought you could, and that you'll have to reconsider your timeline, or even your performance objective. Or, you may realize that you have more time than you thought.

The next step is to look at what you can control in your schedule. Look at the bigger blocks of time you have available: if you have a two- or three-week window to prepare for an event, identify all of the controllable aspects in that time frame. In sport, we will look at a game schedule and search for the gaps where we can add additional loading—meaning, increase the intensity or volume of training—or a longer recovery break. Or, we might look for ways to manipulate our training schedule to better prepare for our objectives, such as identifying periods that allow for more focused interventions, training, strategic work, or rest. Remember, for key moments where you'll have to perform, think about the seventy-two-hour performance window that I explained in the previous chapter, and how you can optimize your readiness and minimize the negative impact of moderators.

From here, look to your weekly and daily commitments and any spaces of time where you can fit in your preparation. This will help you identify the template you have to work with from a planning perspective. Think back to your objective and all of the interventions you identified, and prioritize the top three interventions that you will need to implement to get closer to meeting that objective. Those three interventions are now your scheduling priority for those spaces of time.

Fundamentals First, Marginal Gains Second

In Chapter 6, I told you about Sir David Brailsford's marginal gains approach, which combines small attainable steps as a way to make larger strides. When used appropriately, this approach can be a powerful tool for achieving your goals—whether that's bringing your product to a particular development milestone or, like Brailsford did, turning British Cycling into one of the most powerful cycling programs in the world.

But there is a caveat with the marginal gains approach. It can be very effective in elite cycling, because cycling—especially track cycling—is a very controlled environment. The difference between gold and not medalling at all can be a fraction of a second. When a quarter of a percentage point matters, every tiny, seemingly negligible gain can add up to have a significant impact on the outcome. But in cycling and in every other field, if you're not taking care of the fundamentals, marginal gains will not get you where you need to go.

Yes, the British Olympic cycling team used the marginal gains approach, and yes, it worked well for them—I was at the 2008 Olympics in Beijing working with the Canadian cycling team and I saw the truth of that firsthand. But I also saw that they did not do so at the cost of the basics—they had already taken care of all the fundamentals. The program had talented, committed athletes who came well prepared to deliver the outputs required and were surrounded by quality coaches and support staff. This enabled the marginal gains to have an impact.

Little things don't matter all of the time—they are only impactful when you've already done everything you can to optimize the *big* things. If you focus on the things that can move the dial by a quarter or half a percentage point and neglect the things that can move it by 4, 5, or even 10 percent, you will have a net decrease in performance. It's simple math.

I've listened to many coaches, clients, athletes, and support teams talking about focusing their preparation on marginal gains, and that those small percentage points are going to add up to the difference in output. And in some situations, when they are being strategic and looking to take marginal steps to develop performance over time, this works well. However, when you take significant resources, time, or dollars and direct it at discrete aspects that have a very small impact on output rather than on fundamentals or the bigger blocks, you are going to face unintended consequences. If a developmental cycling team spends tens of thousands of dollars on figuring out the best aerodynamic components in the cyclists' equipment and clothing, they might not have enough money left over to invest in an additional coach who could monitor and oversee their training sessions. If this same team is regularly skipping workouts or the quality of those workouts is poor, it will be a waste of money for them to focus on aerodynamics. I have seen sports teams spend significant sums of money on monitoring technologies that perhaps improve the output by a couple of percentage points, yet the players were not getting top-quality training sessions and coaching to make sure they had the

What preparation will it take for you to win your version of an Olympic medal? There's no one simple answer, **other than a cumulation of everything.**

fundamental technical and tactical skills down. All of this leads to wasted effort, or effort that may not be in any way advantageous for performance impact.

This poor allocation of resources becomes more apparent in the individual realms of personal performance or recreational athletics. Look around, and you will see people spending large amounts of money and time to chase small gains without thinking about how those investments will interact with everything else they're doing. They're looking for marginal gains, often in place of addressing the fundamentals.

Fundamental performance factors account for the majority of performance, so focus your energies on these. Make sure you are addressing the fundamentals first, before spending time and resources on marginal gains. Your priority is gaining the key physical, mental, technical, and tactical skills required to deliver your output. Avoid the temptation to focus your preparation on marginal gains until you are sure you are performing consistently and are addressing the fundamental aspects that you determined are required to deliver your output. Once you are doing those things well, then you can turn your remaining attention and resources toward marginal gains.

Preparing for Moderators

In the last chapter I talked at length about moderators and how they can impact your output. Given that they can have such a significant impact, it is very important to consider them in your planning. I know: it's impossible to prepare for everything, and you could drive yourself crazy trying to cover every possible scenario. So how can you plan for the unpredictable?

What you're really trying to do when you are considering moderators is mitigate your risks to optimize your output. Where I've seen the greatest success is in thinking ahead about the most likely moderators (such as the ones I describe starting on page 124) and then targeting one or two key interventions that will have generally positive impacts across several of those moderators. The further out you can anticipate, the more time you have to plan potential solutions.

When people ask me to name the most important thing you can do to prepare for moderators, my answer is always the same: "It depends." It depends on your individual background, needs, focus, circumstances, and priorities. However, I have observed that the people who are physically fit, have good nutrition habits, and regularly get quality sleep are the ones who tend to handle moderators better. If I had to choose just one thing to minimize the impact of moderators, it would be to improve your aerobic fitness (often referred to as cardiovascular fitness) above the capacity required for your performance objective—and I recommend this not just for athletes, but for anyone working toward a challenging objective. The reason for this is simple. Improved aerobic fitness can positively affect most of the moderators that I described in the previous chapter. It can also positively affect your ability to tolerate load and reduce fatigue, improve your ability to recover, dampen the impact of environmental moderators such as heat and altitude as well as jet lag, and have positive effects on your mood, your ability to handle stress, and your self-efficacy.

SOME KEY BENEFITS OF ENHANCED AEROBIC FITNESS

Improves:

- Work capacity and recovery
- Cardiac function
- HDL ("good") cholesterol
- Immune system function
- Mood and energy levels
- Sleep quality
- Reaction time
- Cognitive function and memory
- Ability to handle stress

Decreases:

- Obesity
- Blood pressure
- Risk of diabetes
- Risk of cardiovascular disease
- Risk of premature death

Any excess aerobic fitness you may have will act as a buffer to protect you when adversity strikes. Aside from a few athletes whose performance output requires a near maximally developed aerobic system, most people have room to improve their aerobic fitness beyond what is required for them to execute their desired performance. When you put in the effort to create that extra aerobic capacity—that added slack—you will find that tasks become easier, recovery becomes faster, and your resistance to fatigue becomes greater. On top of that, the added health benefits of improved aerobic fitness will further support your long-term performance.

Evaluate Your Impact

While there are many ways to design successful plans and interventions, finding the best strategies that work for individuals involves a bit of trial and error. There is no one-size-fits-all solution. So how do you ensure your impact and efforts are positive, or at least stable rather than negative? And how do you minimize time you are spending on interventions that aren't producing results? You do it by identifying the key metrics that are relative to your interventions and objectives, and then measuring them at regular intervals to assess the impacts on the attributes of your profile you are trying to change and the impacts of that change on your ability to deliver the output.

I know that sounds daunting—especially if you are the type of person who is not inclined to be analytical or you think that this measurement process requires sophisticated or expensive equipment and technology. It definitely can but it doesn't always need to. The most important aspect of your evaluation process and metrics is that they are doable, and that they follow the general guidelines I outlined in Chapter 6 for measurement and evaluation.

To evaluate your impact, you can use two different types of metrics: *subjective* measures and *objective* measures. Subjective measures are based on opinions, observations, or some aspect of unquantifiable evidence. While subjective evaluations tend to be less valid, reliable, and sensitive than well-selected objective measures, gathering expert opinion can be quite valuable in assessing aspects that are difficult to measure. Good examples of subjective measures would be when a coach evaluates a player's ability to read the play and make the right decision in the moment of a game, or when a leader is able to determine a culture shift in the organization or the feel of their team's alignment.

Objective measures, meanwhile, require data that are based on quantifiable facts—in other words, the measurement of some attribute that produces a value. A good example of this would be the number of passes completed, the number of sales for a particular territory, or a player's batting average. Each of these is quantifiable and is a fact that is difficult to argue against. But just because they are facts does not mean they are valid or good measures of your output, even if they may seem to be on the surface. It is not uncommon for objective measures to be used inappropriately when evaluating performance.

So, always take the time to assess the objective measures you are using to ensure they are valid in the context in which you are using them.

When you are ready to begin your evaluation process, your first step is to determine whether you are affecting change in the aspect of your profile that you are trying to influence. For example, if you are taking private lessons for shooting in basketball to help you achieve your objective of becoming a starter on your college team, you need to evaluate if you are becoming a better shooter. Similarly, if you are taking a technical course on generating leads so that you can achieve your objective of becoming the top sales performer on your team, you need to evaluate if that course is actually improving your skill in generating leads. Yes, it sounds obvious, but this can be a surprisingly fuzzy area. Learning theory, for example, may not actually improve your application of a skill. Just like a player on a team might be able to learn the tactics and what's required of them, but later they find they can't actually apply it. If your evaluation determines that there has been little to no improvement when compared to the investment of time or other resources, then the next step is to determine if your intervention needs more time to produce change, or if the intervention is in fact the right intervention.

But what if your evaluation of the intervention shows that there has been a positive change? In that case, the next question you need to ask yourself is whether the aspect you have improved is actually translating to an improvement in your performance objective. Does becoming a

Make sure you are addressing the fundamentals first, before spending time and resources on marginal gains.

better shooter lead to you being a starter on your college team? Is the increased lead generation translating to improved sales? If the answer is yes, congratulations: you've focused on an intervention that not only improves your profile but also has a direct impact on your performance output. If the answer is no, that doesn't mean you have wasted your time. Remember: you have actually improved your profile. So, perhaps you simply need a greater change, or perhaps it was an intermediate step and now you need to modify your intervention until it is helping you deliver the output.

It's important to conduct this evaluation process at regular intervals, so you can determine if the interventions are both improving your profile and having a positive impact on your output. This cycle of evaluate, prioritize, and intervene should repeat itself consistently throughout your preparation to ensure you are staying on track.

Preparation in Practice

Leading up to the 2010 Winter Olympic Games in Vancouver, Canada, I worked with the Canadian National Snowboard Team and led their sports science and medicine program. There were great athletes in the program, and it had some success at World Cup and World Championship events, yet it did not win a medal in the last two Olympics. I was asked to join the team in 2007 and contribute to the effort to develop a plan to help the team achieve its goal.

Together, we looked at all aspects of performance and what was going to be required to win in the team's respective speed events. After ensuring that the fundamentals were taken care of—that the athletes had good training, coaching, competition, and recovery—we began preparing for any adverse moderators, like bad weather or a lengthy delay. We also concentrated on taking care of the little details, like goggle management, warming up at the right moments, and having multiple sets of clothing available in case it rained. The team practiced weather strategies over the six months prior to the Games so that they would be ready for any situation. In the end, the athletes were all well prepared, and they did what they had to do on the day. Together, the snowboard cross and alpine snowboard teams won a combined three medals: two gold and one silver.

What preparation will it take for you to win your version of an Olympic medal? There's no one simple answer, other than a cumulation of everything. You work through a process that begins with defining the objective, and you make sure you are honest and clear well in advance so that you can accurately define the output that is required and all the obstacles that potentially stand in the way. For the National Snowboard Team, their objective was to win medals, and their key to that objective was to make sure they could deliver the output required on demand. As a team, we had to look at the athletes' current abilities and identify the priorities in each of the Core 4—the areas of focus for interventions. They spent the time improving their fitness so they could tolerate the increases in on-snow training that was required to refine technical and tactical riding, and so they could adapt to the new technology. We also had to acknowledge that there were certain things we had no control over—moderators like bad weather or long delays—and come up with plans to address and prepare for them as best as we could. Everyone involved knew that the athletes were capable and our expectations were aligned with the output required to win medals. As a team, the athletes delivered on that output—they were high performers.

So, weren't those same objectives just as clear in the eight to ten years prior to the Olympics? Yes, they were. The difference is that, in the years leading up to 2010, everything the coaches, athletes, and support staff did was directly related to producing the output required to win medals. In previous competitions, the team hadn't prepared as far out or focused on as many details as far in advance. This time, we included that preparation in our focus. We tested and trialed approaches and strategies at events in the year leading up to the Games. Of course, even in our painstakingly orchestrated run-up to the 2010 Olympics, we still did things wrong, and, as will always happen, circumstances arose that were unexpected or out of our control. But as a team—coaches, athletes, and staff—we had sat down well in advance and had gone through every possible thing we could think of to limit the challenges and potential negative impacts on performance. We were prepared.

Pursue excellence in your preparation. Manage the things you can control. Build your profile to deliver the required output on demand—that is high performance.

Lesson Learned

Committing to purposeful planning is critical to high performance. Planning out the interventions that will help you deliver the output is more complicated than you think: added effort in one Core 4 area might have a negative impact on another; focusing too closely on one aspect of your overall objective might cause you to fail in another. To create an effective preparation plan, you need to understand net performance impact. You also have to account for moderators and focus on addressing the fundamentals before anything else.

9

Your Integrated Support Team

Everyone needs a support team.

ANYONE WHO has watched a Formula One event knows that the race-car driver—while impressive—is not the only factor in who wins the race. At least once in every Grand Prix session, that driver will need to stop in the pit lane, and that's when you will see a frenetic burst of activity, with twenty or more expert-level individuals working in close proximity and sometimes on top of each other to refuel the tank, repair any damage, change the tires, make adjustments, advise and assess the driver, and more, all at high speed. You can feel the intensity, the focus, and the teamwork as they come together for a collective objective: completing the pit stop as fast as possible so the driver can deliver on the performance objective. They don't work in silos but instead integrate their skill sets, accomplishing feats like delivering a full tire change in under three seconds.

While most people do not (and should not) have a team as intensely kinetic as an F1 driver's surrounding them, high performers do typically have some kind of support team they can call on to help them achieve their objectives, even if it is just one or two people. Everyone needs a support team. It is very rare to see anyone achieve sustainable high performance on their own.

Designing Your Team

When we go to live sports events or watch them on television, we see the individual athletes or teams deliver the performance. We see the coaches on the sidelines providing feedback or making adjustments, and we see the players responding accordingly. What we are watching is the output delivered by those involved in the field of play. But behind these performers is a much larger team, usually called an integrated support team (IST). In sport, in addition to the technical and tactical coaches, ISTs commonly consist of a group of trained and experienced professionals, including an exercise physiologist or exercise scientist, a physician or medical consultant, a dietitian, a psychologist, a physiotherapist, a massage therapist, a strength and conditioning specialist, and others as required. Working with these carefully chosen people increases an athlete's chances of meeting their objectives and achieving success—and on an elite level, they are indispensable.

A support team for personal performance will vary based on the field and objective, but will generally include support for coaching, training, specialized decision-making guidance, technical or tactical skills, mentoring, and expertise. Musicians will work with session players, songwriters, studio managers, producers, sound techs, and audio editors to create an album. An author might draw support and feedback from a mentor or writing group, and will work with editors and designers to create a book. Someone with a heart health issue may have support and guidance from experts like a dietitian and a cardiologist in addition to their general practitioner.

When you start seeking out practitioners, mentors, and other individuals to bring into your personal support team, always remember that an exceptional working relationship is one where you feel listened to and understood. Any practitioners who work closely with you should learn about and get to know you. You will know this is happening when the decisions those experts make, along with how they communicate, the interventions they choose, and what types of additional practitioners or supports they recommend, will all be aligned with you. In sport, if an athlete is detail-oriented and is referred to a support person who is more of a freewheeling spirit, no matter how excellent that practitioner may be, it's not going to work. However, that same practitioner might be a perfect fit for an athlete who doesn't need a high level of focus or detail.

The Pyramid of Attributes

Beyond the need for alignment, there are four fundamental attributes to look for when you are choosing a practitioner or any other kind of support team member: personality, meaningful relationships, knowledge, and expertise. The challenge is that these attributes build on each other—and the more of them a practitioner has, the better they'll be, but the harder they will be to find.

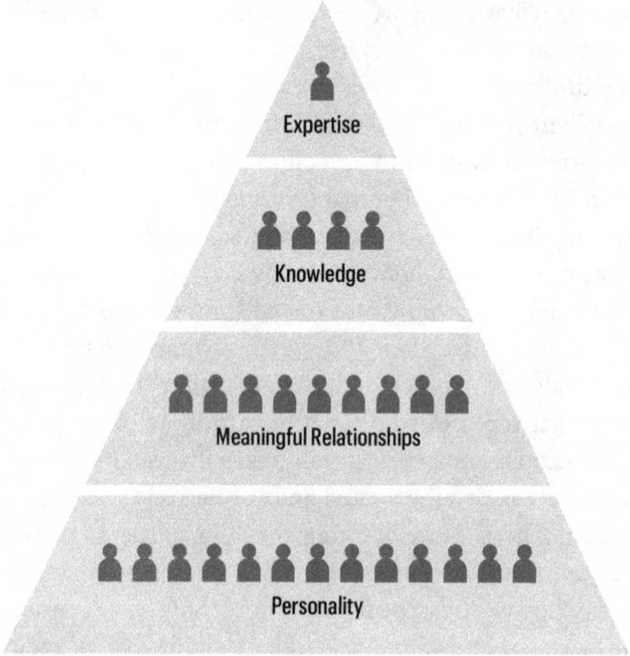

The Pyramid of Attributes

A practitioner cannot build meaningful relationships if they don't have a personality that helps them relate to people, and they can't gain real-world expertise if they don't have knowledge. Your goal as a high performer is to seek out the highest-performing practitioners and supporters you can get—meaning, those people available to you who have the highest number of these attributes that suit your objective. (I will explain this in a bit more detail later.)

Attribute #1: Personality Style

Any practitioner or support team member you choose needs to have a personality style that is appropriate to their job—they must be able to relate to people. This is true of many people, making this attribute both extremely available (which is why it is at the base of the pyramid) and extremely accessible. You might see this attribute take the form of an enthusiastic and understanding personal trainer. Or it may be the coach or teacher whom you enjoy spending time with.

Attribute #2: Meaningful Relationships

The second quality to look for in a support team member is the ability to create meaningful relationships. A practitioner at this level isn't only able to relate to you, they are also able to put you first, to make ethical choices, to make good decisions, and to make sure those decisions benefit you. People who can do these things understand critical thinking and are able to connect with their client to build a meaningful relationship that is valued. These qualities are a little more challenging to find, but are still fairly available.

Attribute #3: Knowledge

An ideal practitioner is well-educated in their particular field. Even if someone on your team is good to work with and good at building supportive and ethically sound relationships, if they are not educated in their specialty they will be limited in their ability to help you reach your objective. The more skills and education you require from them, the further up the pyramid they will be (meaning, the harder for you to access). And knowledge is about more than education, too. It's great if they have an advanced degree or additional certifications in their field, but are they also able to put that learning to work in the real world?

Attribute #4: Expertise

This is the ideal spot on the support team pyramid—but it is also the hardest type of person to find. This is where the experts live. The practitioners here have specialized expertise, along with every other attribute in the pyramid, and they can synthesize those attributes to your benefit. To reach this level requires years of experience in applying their craft and in making decisions in every kind of scenario. That experience is what allows them to better understand which tools to apply in which situations to help you define and deliver your required outputs. These are the professionals that have great personalities, can create meaningful relationships, have extensive knowledge in their subject area, and are very experienced in applying their craft and making decisions in every kind of scenario (and they have a track record of success to prove it). These individuals are the rarest of practitioners, and you are fortunate if you can get them on your team.

The Hiring Process

So, how can you know where a given practitioner falls on the pyramid of attributes before you have worked with them? And how can you evaluate whether that person is a good fit for you, and how well they can meet your needs? You do this by asking the right questions. But the process doesn't start with interviewing the practitioner—it starts with interviewing yourself. Ask yourself questions like:

- What type of person do I best relate to?
- Do I understand the language of this practitioner?
- What specific area of the Core 4 do I need help with?
- What specific skills do I need to learn within that Core 4 factor?
- Can I clearly communicate what I need?
- Do I need someone to "drive the bus" and lead the performance plan to set the direction and keep me accountable? Or do I simply need training that I can schedule on my own terms?

An exceptional working relationship is one where you feel **listened to and understood.**

Once you have taken an honest look at your needs and your ideal personality fit, you will have a better idea of what kind of answers you are looking for when you are ready to meet with potential support team members. Now you can begin your interviews. To determine where a candidate fits on the pyramid of attributes, ask questions such as:

- What is your education and training in this area?
- Tell me about your work history. How much experience do you have with my situation?
- Can you connect me with other clients who can tell me about their experience?
- Do you have experts working within your group? Can you tell me about them?
- Can you work collaboratively with me? How about with other practitioners that I bring on?
- If I want to self-direct my training, will you let me take the lead?
- If I want you to "drive the bus," what will that leadership look like?
- If you are driving the bus, who else will you let on, and will I have the opportunity to assess them?
- How much will this cost?
- What kind of a commitment do you need on my end?
- How will we work together to measure the results?

As you hold this conversation, there are unspoken questions you should be considering as well, and the answers must be found through your observation:

- Are our personalities a good fit?
- Is this person a good individual who is ethically strong?
- Are they focused on my goals, or are they more interested in doing what they think I should focus on?
- Do they have my best interests in mind?
- Will they be able to identify what is best for my performance objectives?
- Will they be able to integrate their work with other practitioners?
- Are the prices for their services aligned with where they sit in the pyramid?

SPEAKING THE LANGUAGES OF YOUR SUPPORT TEAM

Practitioners are trained in specialty boxes. In sport, you may use the services of a strength coach, a rehabilitation specialist, a physiotherapist, a mentor, a coach, a data scientist, a mental training expert, or a dietitian. Many of these people see the world from a single lane of their expertise and may not be able to take in the whole picture. To integrate all of the specialties in your support team—whatever your field—you or your team lead will need to speak the different languages of those disciplines. If you can't, it is going to feel like you've entered a room with five different people who speak five different languages. They may be excellent at what they do, but the communication is going to break down.

The people you work with from the various disciplines should ideally each spend some time working in or with others from fields other than their own. Modern-day practitioners have to be able to understand other perspectives. For example, people often speak about "fitness." What is fitness? We all have our different opinions on what fitness means. A coach will have a different definition from a therapist or an expert with a physiology or strength perspective. We need to be able to speak with a common understanding. Multilingual practitioners—the ones who can see perspectives other than their own and are able to understand the terminologies used in different fields—are better able to work with other types of practitioners. And practitioners who have a systems approach to performance are better able to integrate with others and effectively apply their own trades.

Who Do You Actually Need?

Let's step back for a moment: before you even begin interviewing candidates, it is important to assess where you are at in meeting your goals and objectives, and to determine what level of help you need, and who that might be. Depending on the need and performance objective, if you can't find the right person, you may be better off not hiring anyone and putting your resources elsewhere.

In sport, if a team I am working with only needs a massage therapist to do massage for relaxation, the depth and quality of assessment is not as important. On the other hand, if they need a therapist to do high-quality massage work in a heavy training load phase with an athlete who needs to have quality tissue work done on a regular basis, then we will have to look higher up the pyramid and invest more resources to secure the right person.

Give yourself permission to create your own plan and to identify and be comfortable with your current needs. A support team can be several people, or it might only be you and one other person. The people you need now might be different from those you need in the future—accept that you don't have to do everything all at once. Later, you might need a high level of technical expertise in a specific area; for now, you may only need someone who has an enthusiastic personality and who will keep you accountable to your performance plan. At each stage, look for people on the highest relevant point in the pyramid you can find within the resources you are able to commit. And, no matter their level, look for people who are trustworthy, who have a personality that fits with yours, who have applied experience, and who like to collaborate.

It comes down to listening to yourself. You have the answers about what you need or don't need. Surround yourself with skillful people and experts where you need

The process doesn't start with interviewing the practitioner—**it starts with interviewing yourself.**

them. Be purposeful about who you bring on to your team. Make sure that anyone you bring on is aligned with your objective and is supporting you to achieve it. All successful people work with a support team that is strategic and realistic and aligned with their goals and with their organization's goals. Ensure that you have strong leadership, either within yourself to implement your plan, or as external support to keep you accountable. Building an appropriate and committed personal performance team will help you focus and maintain your optimal performance and support all your efforts and work.

Fitting Your Team into Your Performance Plan

Ideally, your team members are knowledgeable and experienced and work collaboratively together openly and honestly to focus on optimal performance. They evaluate your personal data and goals and put together a set of clear, strategic, and realistic performance recommendations for you. Having access to meaningful and purposeful metrics that are individual to you and are performance focused will allow you to see where you are at in terms of meeting your objective. It also helps you set future goals.

The data analysis and insights your team provides you with should tell you what you need to do differently to improve your performance. Make sure that any metrics you and your team decide to use follow the guidelines I outlined in Chapters 6 and 8. The decisions you make together should be evidence based and should use existing knowledge and critical thinking. You start with a theoretical basis for why an intervention may or may not work, then you examine what makes it work, or not, in real life.

Working with team members who don't know what direction you are heading in together is challenging. Someone on your team—you or the team lead—needs to have a vision and direction on how the various pieces of your program work together. In sport, everyone, including the coach, practitioners, and support staff, has to be able to sit down and decipher which top two or three pieces are going to have the biggest net impact on performance, keeping in mind the resources it will take and what is feasible. The same holds true in your personal performance.

Everyone has different needs and aspects that influence their performance, such as talent, training, history, psychology, and current health status. Make sure your team looks at your gaps. It's important that they work together to focus their support on producing a net performance impact—they cannot be working in silos. If they think you need work in a certain factor, but doing that work will negatively impact a bigger priority, will they be willing to let that piece go? If I'm working with an athlete who needs to get faster, but achieving that goal will take four training sessions a week and will reduce their ability to do tactical training, will that have a negative net performance impact? If you go to the gym five days a week for the physical and mental benefits, but that time away is undermining a critical and time-sensitive work project, have you accurately calculated the net performance impact? The equation is surprisingly simple: if something is not having a net performance impact that's positive, then it's negative. Make sure that your support team's impact on your performance is positive, or at the very least stable. Your team shouldn't be a disruption. They should provide support in an environment that allows you to be successful.

THE 5 PHASES OF CRITICAL THINKING

Accurately defining your required output and building a plan to achieve it demands the ability to think critically about the factors and decisions that influence your performance—in other words, the context of your actions and decisions. Over the years I spent learning the five key phases of critical thinking from Dr. Howie Wenger, I began to comprehend their importance in understanding challenges and designing solutions for clients. Everyone on your support team should understand the need for a critical thinking framework, and be able to implement it in a cohesive way at every stage of your preparation plan.

1. **GATHERING:** Understand your questions and gather the latest information, research, and theoretical reasoning about it. Using credible sources, try to get as much information as you can that is related to your performance objective, defining the output required, your profile, and ways to improve your ability to deliver output. Beware of anecdotes and pseudoscience.

2 **PROCESSING:** Take all of the evidence, data, and information you have gathered and adapt it into the format you need—whether that is through direct calculation, categorizing, or entry into a specific analytical program. Make sure the information is in a usable format that will allow you to analyze it relative to your performance objective and profile.

3 **ANALYZING:** Study and synthesize the information until you understand what it means as a whole. Review the information and data and draw connections between different pieces. Look for patterns and causal relationships within the information with respect to performance. Are the gaps that you perceive real or are they just perceived? Remember that correlation does not mean causation.

4 **CONTEXTUALIZING:** Examine the synthesized information both within the context in which you operate and within the context from which it came. Ask questions about the information and what might be influencing it. Ask specifically how the information is relevant to you and your objectives.

5 **COMMUNICATING:** Rearticulate the information and your findings based on those contexts. Then, put the information into simple words so that you can communicate it clearly. You should be able to understand and articulate to others your objectives, the output that is required, and what you need to do to get there. You should be able to communicate this with everyone on your support team.

When everything in your life is going according to plan, it can be easy to fall into the belief that you don't need any help from anyone.

When Your Support Team Really Matters

When everything in your life is going according to plan, it can be easy to fall into the belief that you don't need any help from anyone to get where you want to go. But when unexpected events arise—as they always do—that's when you will feel the presence (or absence) of a support team in the most profound way.

You might get injured. Your business might come under threat, or some funding you expected might fall through. There might be a major economic downturn in your country (or the world), or you might face a family or personal crisis that takes up all of your emotional and physical energy. When events like these arise seemingly out of nowhere, you need to have an established team at the ready who can support you. Their expertise and perspective can help you put aside stress and panic and get to work on adapting your plan and minimizing any lost progress. They will have clarity on what interventions are best for you or your business, how you will respond to those interventions, what you have capacity for, and even your likes and dislikes. They will already know your history and will already be aligned with your objectives, and they can help support you in other areas that may not be impacted by the interruption. If the crisis demands support from other professionals, they can advise you on who to bring in, and may even have existing relationships with those experts. You will waste less time in trying to figure out who you need and how to get access to them, and you will be able to adjust your plan and recover from the disruption more quickly. And as your support team takes on the work of adjusting your plan, you focus on the work of recovering from your crisis.

One afternoon I was sitting at home when my phone rang. A client I had been working with for several years had crashed on his mountain bike—he had suffered several injuries, including the fracture of two vertebrae in his neck. Over the time this client and I had worked together, we had developed an extensive support team, including a doctor, a physical therapist, a personal trainer, and a physiologist, plus five or so additional support people who we could bring on as needed. Some of those practitioners had come and gone from the team over the years, but we had always ensured continuity in programming, and all of the people we drew on for support were already comfortable working collaboratively.

This client trained regularly to stay fit and healthy, was an active owner of a large company, and had a family that he spent lots of time with. That afternoon, his life changed immediately. And, just as immediately, those of us on his support team went into action. There was little we could do in a hands-on sense for the time that he was in the hospital and under the care of his surgeon, but from the moment of that first phone call we were already at work, adapting his plan and making sure that the additional support people would be there when we needed them. Together with his doctor and his surgeon, we designed a safe, effective, and informed recovery plan that we communicated with his team, and arranged for regular physical therapy to optimize both his recovery and his return to his original performance plan.

Within four weeks of his accident, the client was doing light hikes in gentle terrain to help maintain his lower-body muscle mass. To help with his mobility and range of motion, we brought in an additional manual therapist with soft tissue expertise. Within six weeks he was out of his neck brace. At week seven, we began to increase the difficulty of his hikes, and we added in stationary bike rides two to three times per week. During all this time, we were working with the client and the various practitioners on our recovery team to adapt and integrate his program and plan so that it was appropriate for his stage of recovery. Long before the accident, the client had booked a trip to Italy—he had always wanted to ride his road bike in the Dolomites. At week ten after his accident, the client was on that plane with full medical clearance. He spent a week in Italy, riding his bike for up to 80 kilometers a day through the mountains.

Unexpected events will happen. The next one that fate brings to your door might not be as significant as a broken neck, but it could still upend your performance plan and impact your output if you haven't taken steps to create a support network. Your team doesn't have to be extensive or expensive, but if you want to achieve your objective no matter what comes your way, you have to have people you can count on in a crisis. Develop those relationships before you need them—you'll be grateful that you did.

Lesson Learned

Every high performer needs a support team. When you are assessing practitioners, coaches, and people who provide other forms of support, honestly assess your needs, and look for people as high up on the pyramid of attributes as suits the level of your objective. Ask the right questions, employ critical thinking, and make sure that all of your support team members can and will work well together and with your personal needs and priorities. And, most importantly, have them in place before any unexpected event can upend your plans.

10

Designing Your Performance Road Map

A purposeful performance roadmapping process is circular: it consistently returns to your priorities and to your why, and then leads outward to action.

EVERY CLIENT I have ever worked with has been unlike any other client. Their stories are always unique and our discussions always vary. The questions we cover will always lead down their own path as we work together to determine their why, to figure out what they really need to work on, and to understand what will be required for them to achieve their objective. Sometimes it will be an iterative process where we jump around, and other times it will be very linear. But however different the various roads to a client's objectives are from each other, the same five key milestones always appear. Each milestone represents an action, and they are all necessary steps in achieving any challenging objective.

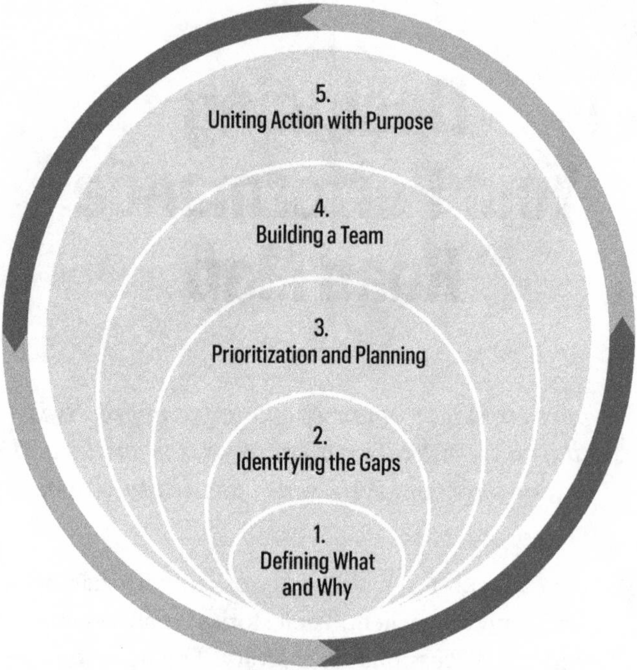

The Performance Road Map

The first four of these milestones are everything you have read in this book so far. The last one, number five, is what I am going to talk about at the end of this book.

Together, they create a road map that anyone who is interested in high performance can follow—no matter what your goal is, or how you as an individual plan to get there.

Everyone speaks their own language when it comes to their personal vision for themselves, and unfortunately there is no way for me to speak to you directly in the language that is unique to you through the one-way medium that is a book. But if I were there with you right now, these five action areas are what we would talk about first. Every experience I've had in working with high performers—both in sport and in the executive world—has involved each of these components. I don't think I have ever seen a case of sustained success that has not built in each of these five fundamentals at some level in the process of reaching and maintaining that success.

The Five Key Actions in Your Performance Road Map

Remember, this five-stage process to achieve high performance will be the same regardless of whether you're a developing athlete, a professional player, a C-suite executive, or a working professional trying to manage a career with home life. The pathway in between these milestones is the personal part: it's how each of the strategies and considerations you have read about in this book relate to you. To help you lock in your milestones, let's take a moment to briefly recall and summarize each of the five key actions you will need in order to keep yourself moving in the right direction.

Key Action #1: Defining What and Why

Be very clear on your performance objective. It is important that you both understand and are comfortable with your why. The answers to the "why questions" I described on page 91 should drive every single decision you make regarding what you're doing and how you engage at work, at home, or in sport. To first articulate your performance objective and then to prioritize the specific actions and interventions, you have to understand what is important to you. To get there, you cannot skip that process of questioning: Why are you doing what you're doing? What are your true priorities?

Key Action #2: Identifying the Gaps

The next step is to assess what's required to achieve your objective and how your Core 4 profile compares to those requirements—this is the auditing process I described in Chapter 6. If your audit is not honest, your ability to achieve your objective will be based on false assumptions. It's especially important to examine the controllable and uncontrollable factors that influence your efforts, because effort needs to be directed to the factors you can control if you are to achieve your objective and perform optimally. Do an honest audit of what's required to achieve your objectives. Don't forget to consider the moderators that may influence your output: Are there ways in which you can address the ones that you can expect to experience regularly? Should those moderators be part of your required output? Take a look at any problems or gaps that are occurring with your performance output and consider metrics or ways to measure performance—to track how you're doing in meeting your performance objective.

Key Action #3: Prioritization and Planning

Be purposeful. Prioritize the actions that are directly related to your overall objective and that will result in you being able to produce the required output. If you need to, remind yourself of your why so that you understand your true motivation and can base your decisions around it. If you are only doing what someone else is telling you to do, it is probably not aligned with your objectives, and it definitely won't last. If you own your performance and you have done the work to gain awareness over your why, then it becomes sustainable. Your time is limited—just as it is for everyone. Each of us only gets twenty-four hours a day, seven days a week. It's how we prioritize those hours that keeps us on the path to achieving our performance objectives. Think of your strengths and the things you can improve on. Which ones will have a bigger impact on your performance objective? Which need to come first? Be aware of the trade-offs, and work toward optimizing your net performance impact. Use metrics to track how you're doing from an objective perspective. And never forget to put the fundamentals first—marginal gains are only useful if you are adequately addressing the factors with the biggest impact on your output.

Key Action #4: Building a Team

Surround yourself with good people that you can empower and trust. Do you feel understood and respected? Optimal performance is never a one-person show. Behind every consistently high-performing athlete is a team of coaches, practitioners, and support staff—just as every high performer in every field has a team of mentors, advisors, and skilled assistants that allows them to achieve. Identify the areas where you need support and which areas you can realistically manage on your own. Who is on your "team," and what roles do they fill? What roles need to be filled with more expertise, to strengthen that team? Remember: depending on your situation, a team can be as small as one or two people. Whoever they are, make sure that your personalities align or complement each other, that you all understand who is driving the plan and who is following it, and that each individual can work effectively with everyone else you have surrounded yourself with.

Key Action #5: Uniting Action with Purpose

This is exactly what we will cover in the final chapter that follows, but I want to quickly address it here because it is an indispensable part of your performance road map. Being accountable to a plan and a process and acting with purpose are critical parts of success. You must understand that *you* are in control. Acting with purpose will bring you a greater level of acceptance of and willingness to participate in the programs and processes that are necessary for your objectives. Intentional action connects

As you progress,
your priority gaps may
change, and so should
your interventions . . .
**It is an iterative,
ongoing process.**

your efforts to a goal, and to your performance objective. Hold yourself accountable and review your plan and progress regularly. Are you getting closer to being able to produce the output required for your performance objective?

Purposeful Roadmapping

I am not going to tell you that this is an easy process. You have to think deeply about how each of these key action areas relates to you and ask yourself the questions in this book. Once you're exhausted from asking those questions, dive into a deeper layer and ask them again. When the answers remain the same every time you ask the questions, you're as deep as you need to go.

While I would typically go through this road map the first time in a linear process, the intent is not to do each milestone once and consider yourself done. A purposeful performance roadmapping process is circular: it consistently returns to your priorities and to your why, and then leads outward to action. You will move through this orbit repeatedly until you have achieved your performance objective. First, you clearly and correctly identify your objectives, then you audit and assess what's required to achieve them, and then you establish direction and priorities. Focus your efforts in an integrated way and prioritize those efforts by applying the strategies and interventions that are appropriate for you. Build your team with appropriate practitioners that suit your needs. Revisit and evaluate your profile relative to the outputs required and determine if you're making progress. If you are, keep going. If you're not, reassess your interventions and determine if they are appropriate. As you progress, your priority gaps may change, and so should your interventions. You may have to go back and redefine the output required as your objective changes, or reprioritize your interventions once you've enhanced your profile. It is an iterative, ongoing process.

Do you remember Susan, our senior manager from Chapter 3? New circumstances have arisen for Susan, and she must handle them with a strategic approach so that she can continue to be a high performer and deliver her desired output in a sustainable way. Over the weeks and months since we last met her, her required output in her role at the accounting firm continued to change. Now, it is once again time for her to go back and re-evaluate her why and revisit her priorities, establish her objective, and audit her profile and the output, and then plan accordingly.

Each time Susan does this, she needs to think about why she loves the things she loves when she's at work. Why does she want to do this work? Does she value advising clients and solving problems? Does she enjoy the opportunities that come with travel? If she decides to continue with significant travel, then she needs to consider her Core 4 gaps and think about who she currently has and who she needs on her support team. Then, she needs to align her actions with her purpose so that she can plan and prepare by putting in the hard work in strategic ways to produce the output required to meet her objective.

Susan, in this case, is you, in whatever role you have now, and for whatever objective is in your sights. And she is also you in whatever your role and objective looks like three months, a year, five years from now. This five-point road map is a path to your goal, and as things change, you need to revisit these key steps to ensure your actions are aligned with your objective.

Lesson Learned

Performance is not meandering, it is a journey with a destination—and to get to any destination you need a road map. What your road map looks like will be unique to you and to your objective, but to take you there effectively, it must have five key milestones: defining what you want to achieve and why, identifying the gaps between what you have and what you need in order to get there, prioritizing and planning the interventions that will close those gaps, building a team to help you close them effectively, and, finally, uniting action with purpose. Creating this map is a repeating, circular process: inward to your why, and then outward to your action.

11

Uniting Action with Purpose

We don't have control over outcomes.
We only have control over how we prepare
and execute on demand—our output.

SOME YEARS ago I began working with a hockey player who had already played in more than 500 NHL games over the course of his career. He had achieved great success in the early stages of his career: being named a league all-star, winning an individual NHL award and team MVP, playing in the Stanley Cup Finals. Now, he was coming off an injury-plagued season and multiple surgeries, and he was looking to get back to the same level he had been playing at before. His why was very clear to him—he wanted to compete at the highest level in the sport he loved for as long as he could. He also really valued the camaraderie of his teammates and the challenge of being prepared as a team each night when they stepped onto the ice. This is what drove him each day, regardless of the outcome.

Don't get me wrong, he loved to win—but that wasn't his only driver. When I asked him about his objectives, he told me that he wanted to excel at a personal level, to have another chance to play with his team in a Stanley Cup game, and to once again be an all-star and get nominated for an NHL award. When I asked him if he had control over all those objectives, he told me that, deep down, he knew that he didn't; the only control he had was over how he prepared and executed what he needed to do to excel at a personal level. His mindset had shifted from outcome-focused objectives to one focused on the required output that he needed to deliver: to lead by example by delivering his skill set night in and night out at his highest level.

After we talked a little more, it became clear that this athlete's biggest hurdle was staying injury free and being well prepared physically to average twenty-plus minutes per night over an eighty-two-game regular season, plus up to twenty-eight games in the playoffs. He still had all the mental, technical, and tactical skills required to deliver the output, but now he had to rethink his physical preparation.

So, for the rest of that off-season, he completely changed his approach. He focused on his performance objective and the output required to achieve it. In previous seasons, his training focus was on lifting weights to be strong and doing sport-specific conditioning on the ice. But now, he was surrounding himself with an integrated team of professionals. We helped him focus on movement technique and his overall capacity to tolerate load and to maintain his quality of movement under fatigue. We worked on integrating his team and his plan and made sure that his physical therapists, skate coaches, strength coaches, and physiologist were working together. At times, we included a dietitian and a mental performance coach. Each of these individuals was connected to the athlete's overall plan and worked together to support him. He had to learn to integrate his new movement patterns into his technical aspects of skating, shooting, and puck protection.

Shortly afterward, he was traded to a team that had only made the playoffs twice in the previous four years and had not won a single series—it was a great example of how a performance can be influenced by factors that are outside of your control. Still, he kept up with his plan, maintaining his focus on what was required to deliver the output throughout the season. Sometimes we had to modify his plan based on his needs and other factors outside of his control, but his support team provided him with continuity in preparing for his performance objective following the trade. We evaluated his progress on his goals relative to his objective and his role with his new team, working with them to adjust as needed. He continued to work on his movement strategies and on maintaining his capacity to tolerate load, and he kept a focus on quality recovery sessions, seeing improvements not only in the individual traits of his profile, but also in how that translated to his ability to deliver output. He started to become stronger and was feeling better on the ice, and over the season he was able to play twenty-plus minutes night in and night out while traveling from city to city. In all, he played a total of ninety-seven regular season and playoff games, missing only one game due to illness.

Over the next several years, we'd regularly revisit this athlete's objectives. We'd identify gaps, prioritize, plan, and update his support team as needed so that he was always acting with purpose. As an athlete, he was committed: he put in the hard work and remained focused on his objectives. He never did get to play for another Stanley Cup. But by setting clear performance objectives and focusing on the output required for him to achieve those objectives, he helped that team to two conference final playoff appearances. He also earned another all-star appearance and two more nominations for individual awards over the next four years.

Match Your Expectations to Your Profile

What happens when you deliver on what you believe is the required output and still don't achieve your objective? Does it mean you were not a high performer?

No it does not. Remember, performance is output, not outcome. But if you deliver the required output and still do not achieve your original objective, you do need to ask yourself why. Often, it will be something that is out of your control—a bad call by a referee, a flight delay, a decision that somebody else made. Barring that uncontrollable factor, your output would have achieved the objective. Once in a while, it won't. *But*, sometimes it might highlight a gap you couldn't see before. Perhaps the required output has changed since you did your audit. Perhaps, during the lead-up to the event, a strong new competitor arrived—if you had been given the chance to factor that in, you would have known you needed to up the required output. Or perhaps you made an error in your original assessment of what was required. High performers are very comfortable with knowing two seemingly conflicting facts at once: that they had prepared themselves as best they could, and that they did not accomplish their objective. That is not complacency. That is a growth mindset.

Regardless of the result, high performers always ask the same question: "What did I learn from this performance?" The answer helps them understand their strengths and gaps, and it allows them to identify whether the required output is within their current reach, or if they need to continue to develop their profile. It is this approach that facilitates sustainable high performance on demand.

It's natural for us to put all of our hopes and intentions on a single outcome: that position in the C-suite, that sales figure, that multimillion-dollar buyout, that medal on a lanyard, or that cup hoisted over your head. But when you can focus on output instead of outcome, you will be better able to evaluate whether or not you had a

Focus on the output required to achieve your objective, and you will take control of your performance and increase the likelihood of success.

good performance. Were you able to deliver the expected output you prepared your profile for? And were you able to do it on demand?

What's important to remember is that this self-analysis matters even when you *do* achieve a given objective. You may perform very well, but at the same time know that your ability to deliver the required output needs to improve. As you continue to prepare and develop your Core 4 profile to get closer to the required output for your objective, your expectations for your performance will increase. Only when your profile is able to produce the required output should you expect to deliver that output.

I'll say it again: human performance is not an outcome but an output. Outcomes are something we can't control. What we can control is how we prepare and execute on demand—our output. If you are working only to achieve a specific outcome, you might do everything right and still never achieve that objective.

And this doesn't change depending on who you are. The same factors will drive a successful performance regardless of the arena or sector you're in or whether you're an athlete, an artist, a musician, or an executive. Focus on the output required to achieve your objective, and you will take control over your performance and increase the likelihood of success. Be honest with yourself as to why your objective is your objective. If you can understand your why and align your actions to your purpose, you will stay connected to the work of preparing for and becoming a high performer.

Own Your Performance

I acknowledge that I'm a white male from the middle class and my exposures may not be the same as someone else's. My background, approaches, and experiences have influenced how I handle things, and your background, approaches, and experiences will influence yours. But I do believe that unpacking the why behind the things that you do is a universal foundation in terms of delivering on the necessary outputs to achieve what you want to achieve. It is a necessary step in defining that objective and prioritizing what is important to you, whether that relates to purposeful performance in sport, at work, at home, or in all of these areas.

There are many factors that will influence your individual performance. Optimal performance requires the integration of physical, mental, technical, and tactical skills; nutrition for sustained energy; and rest and recovery to avoid fatigue. Everything is interrelated, and nothing occurs in isolation. Once you understand your own, personal, unique performance objective—your why—you can then prioritize and be strategic with where you put your energy and effort, to do the right things at the right time. Spend the time up front to clearly define your goals and objectives. Work hard to clearly articulate what you really want to achieve and determine how best to meet those goals. When you have done this work and it is time to create your plan, include benchmarks and an ongoing monitoring process so you can track your progress.

You will always be challenged by external circumstances or events that you cannot dictate. Remember that life happens, circumstances change, and you will sometimes need to adapt your plan so you can use your resources efficiently. Consider the factors that influence performance from an integrated, critical thinking perspective. Most importantly, don't become married to your plan: refusing to vary your path is not always a productive way to move forward. Leading up to that famous World Cup race, Finn Iles had all the will, the commitment, and the support he needed to become the best possible mountain biker he could be, and he did everything he needed to do to prepare himself to deliver the required output. But he couldn't stop his chain from breaking in a freak accident during the actual race. And he couldn't control the competition, either: if Laurie Greenland had gone just a little faster, Finn might have come home with silver, not gold, despite having executed the ride of his life. But even if one of those outcomes had come to pass instead of his victory, Finn's performance was always under his control.

High performers still perform well even in the face of unexpected and negative events. They set performance objectives for themselves, and they control what they can control. For what they can't control, they control how they respond instead. They understand that performance is all about preparation. They don't work alone, but instead surround themselves with a team of people who can support their efforts to reach their goals and help them drive personal and professional performance.

If you're doing something that's not aligned with your purpose, environment, and personality, it won't last. If you own your performance, it becomes achievable.

Understand that it's okay to *not* do something sometimes. Prioritizing your time inevitably means that some things will fall by the wayside—no one can target everything, all the time. Remember, we each only get so many hours in the day and so many days in the year. What matters is how we prioritize those moments. What you want to do and don't want to do is up to you. What are your priorities right now? What is important to you? How much do you want something? What are your action plans for mitigating risks and mistakes and undesirable circumstances or worst-case scenarios?

What I want you to do now is look forward, not backward—so as I conclude this book, I am not going to offer you a final "lesson learned." Instead, I ask you to take a moment to think about your own next chapter. What happens from here in your story is for you to write. So write it. It's time for you to execute.

Acknowledgements

THIS BOOK WOULD NOT exist if it were not for the unwavering support of my life partner and best friend Trina. She has been with me on this entire journey, from keeping sanity in our family while I was away for weeks on end supporting athletes to managing and driving this book project from the beginning. Trina, your support and encouragement along the way have shaped and influenced the thoughts presented in this book. I'm forever grateful.

Thank you to both of our children, Kira and Nathan. First, for inspiring me to be my best self as both a father and role model. Second, for being honest with me when I fall short on delivering my best output! It is this open honesty from people we trust that helps us grow, and I am thankful that you feel comfortable in letting me know.

Thank you to the mentors who have shaped my perspective on integrated performance output and the "art" of applying science to practice, particularly Howie Wenger, Gord Sleivert, and Don McKenzie.

Thank you to the colleagues, coaches, and athletes in high-performance sport whom I've had the opportunity to learn from and work with. There are too many to mention individually, but each one of you has contributed in your own way and has taught me lessons on the importance of individualizing solutions, all while challenging me to rethink performance.

To the clients and friends I've learned lessons from and worked with who strive for sustained high performance, performance on demand, and excellence in achieving their performance objectives: thank you!

Thank you to the publishing team at Page Two Books. As I do in high performance, I surrounded myself with a team of experts to bring this book to production. Page Two operates similarly to an integrated support team in high-performance sport and works collaboratively to maintain optimal performance in the publishing world, listening to their authors and helping them reach their publishing goals. Your personality style, ability to develop a meaningful relationship with us, knowledge, and experience created the perfect team to help support this output to achieve our objective. Thank you!

Optimize Output
and Rethink Performance

Thank you for reading ***Output: Optimizing Your Performance with Lessons Learned from Sport***. If you would like to continue this journey, here are a few steps you can take.

Get copies for your team or organization. If you're interested in having a positive net performance impact at work, bring this book to your team or organization. Bulk discounts and special offers, including custom editions that include a foreword from your leadership team, can be arranged. Email **contact@resync.ca.**

Invite Ben to your event. Interested in a speaker for your event, keynote, or retreat who can engage, inspire, and challenge people to optimize their performance? Ben can help your attendees rethink performance for a net positive performance impact. Email **contact@resync.ca.**

Like this book. If you enjoyed *Output*, please share it with a friend or tell someone about it. Leave a review at your preferred retailer, or join the conversation on social media with other high performers with **#HighPerformance.**

Connect further. Visit **Resync.ca**, connect with Ben on LinkedIn at **linkedin.com/in/bensporer**, or send a note to **contact@resync.ca.** For more information on bulk orders and speaking engagements, visit **www.output-book.com.**

PHOTO: BROOKE MCALLISTER

About the Author

BEN SPORER, PHD, is a performance consultant with twenty-five years of experience working in elite sport and human performance. He spent over a decade with the Canadian Sport Institute holding a number of roles, including senior physiologist and head of performance and research. He is an accomplished physiologist and leader of multidisciplinary integrated support teams at summer and winter Olympic Games and at World Cup and World Championship events, and he is the founder of Resync, a boutique consultancy providing integrated performance solutions to high-performance sports organizations, teams, athletes, and corporate clients. Ben is an adjunct professor at the University of British Columbia and the vice-president of performance strategy for the Vancouver Whitecaps Football Club. He has published dozens of peer-reviewed journal articles and mentors graduate students and practitioners in applied sport sciences, and he translates that scientific and practical background across many fields in his executive and performance strategy consulting.

Printed in the USA
CPSIA information can be obtained
at www.ICGtesting.com
LVHW091329021123
762340LV00004B/165

9 781774 584248